# this
# was
# expo

McClelland and Stewart Limited | Illustrated Books Division

# this was expo

written by **Robert Fulford** | photographed by John de Visser  Harold Whyte  Peter Varley

**The author, Robert Fulford,**
spent four months at Expo as the special
correspondent of the Toronto *Star*. In
his daily column, he usually discusses
books and art. Now 35, he has been writing
for 17 years; he is married to a
journalist and they have two children.

**The photographers**

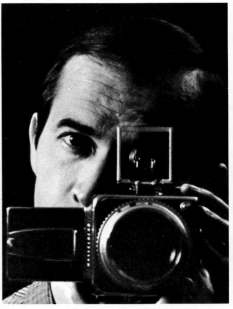

John de Visser came to Canada from Holland
in 1952 and quickly won a reputation
as one of the country's best photographers.

Peter Varley, 46, began his distinguished
career on the West Coast at 14. He is the
son of Group of Seven's Frederick Varley.

Harold Whyte travels out of Toronto on
assignments for Canada's top magazines.
His hobby is electronic colour analysis.

**Table of contents**

McClelland and Stewart Limited,
Illustrated Books Division.
150 Simcoe St., Toronto 1, Ont., Canada

**Publisher** Jack McClelland
**Editorial Director** Pierre Berton
**Editor** Leslie F. Hannon
**Art Director** Hugh Michaelson
**Assistant Art Director** Nick Milton
**Designer** William Fox
**Picture Editor** Linda Knelman
**Assistant Picture Editor** Bill Brooks
**Assistant Editor** Clement Chapple
**Executive Assistant** Ennis Halliday

This volume was designed by Nick Milton

# Introduction

## *A heaven-storming ambition*

World's fairs are about the future, and the great exposition which took place on the man-made islands in the St. Lawrence River in the summer of 1967 was about the future of Canada as well as the future of science, architecture, education and cinematography. No one knows yet whether Expo 67 permanently altered the course of Canadian life, but there was the sense, during that remarkable summer, that as a people we might never be the same again.

On opening day, April 28, Peter Newman of the Toronto *Star* wrote in his syndicated column: "The cannonade of fireworks which marked the opening of Expo . . . may in retrospect turn out to have been one of those rare moments that change the direction of a nation's history . . . This is the greatest thing we have ever done as a nation and surely the modernization of Canada – of its skylines, of its styles, its institutions – will be dated from this occasion and from this fair . . . The more you see of it, the more you're overwhelmed by a feeling that if this is possible, that if this little sub-arctic, self-obsessed country of 20,000,000 people can put on this kind of show, then it can do almost anything."

That feeling – not only of an accomplishment in hand, but of even greater accomplishments to come – lasted all through the six months of Expo's existence, and among some of us it lives yet. It seemed to me to mark the end of Little Canada, a country afraid of its own future, frightened of great plans. Despite the spectre of French-Canadian separatism that haunted Canada through the early and middle 1960s, Expo seemed to suggest that we were now entering a new and happier period in our history. Millions of Canadians must have shared this view, because everywhere you went that summer you encountered the same reaction: *we* had done this, *we* had accomplished this much. Canadians knew that the world's view of our country was quickly changing – the foreign press and television, the foreign visitors, told us so every day – but what was more important was that Expo brought us together for the first time in mutual appreciation and celebration of all our talents. We discovered ourselves.

In this light perhaps the most remarkable fact about Expo is that it almost didn't happen. Only forty-two months before opening day, people across

Canada were talking publicly and seriously about the possibility of killing the fair. "The simplest solution is to call off the whole thing," wrote the financial editor of the Toronto *Star* in September, 1963. This was not an isolated attitude. Some of the ministers in Lester Pearson's five-months-old Federal Government were even then urging the Prime Minister to abandon Expo. George Hees, a former Conservative minister, who was an Expo director in 1963, was to say later: "It was my opinion that there wasn't the slightest chance for Expo. Our chances were zero, nil." And Hees is considered an *optimist*.

That autumn, when the decision was finally made to go ahead, and the pessimists' views were permanently set aside, the governing factor was perhaps not so much confidence in Expo's future as the knowledge that it would probably be more embarrassing to retreat than to proceed.

The minority Pearson government, sworn in on April 22, 1963, inherited Expo from John Diefenbaker's regime. It inherited a mess – a mess of the kind typically produced by more than one level of government participating in a single enterprise. Expo was a project of three governments – Canada, Quebec Province, and Montreal – but of these only two finally counted in the politics of the affair: Mayor Jean Drapeau's Montreal administration and the Diefenbaker and later Pearson governments in Ottawa. The story of the tangle the Liberals confronted in 1963 began at least five years before.

In 1958 a Conservative senator, Mark Drouin, came back from the world's fair in Brussels with the idea that Canada should have a universal exhibition in 1967, to celebrate the 100th birthday of Confederation. The idea grew in Ottawa, and elsewhere. It was briefly discussed in Toronto, then rejected by city politicians. In Montreal, however, Mayor Sarto Fournier liked the idea and began to campaign for it. The Canadian government applied, at the International Exhibitions Bureau in Paris, for the right to hold the most ambitious kind of fair, a first-category exhibition (defined officially as one at which various countries construct their own pavilions and which "constitutes a living testimony to the contemporary epoch"). The Soviet Union, which was to celebrate its 50th anniversary the same year Canada celebrated its 100th, applied for the same right. Since two such fairs can't be held in the same year, Canada had to lobby against the Soviets, and the Soviets won (by a vote of sixteen member countries to fourteen, Byelorussia and the Ukraine voting on the Soviet side). But within two years Moscow had changed its mind, apparently because of the staggering costs. By that time Jean Drapeau was mayor of Montreal, and he set out to win the fair for his city. A federal M.P. from British Columbia was later to ask in the Commons whether Canada was building a monument to Drapeau; the answer, as it turned out, was "Yes."

Drapeau went to Europe to gauge the chances of a Canadian application and came home satisfied. He persuaded Prime Minister John Diefenbaker to make a fresh application; according to one story, his letter to Diefenbaker said an exhibition would promote Canadian unity. Ottawa applied again, and on November 13, 1962, the International Bureau granted Canada the right to hold the Western Hemisphere's first exhibition in the first category.

Then began the friction, not between Drapeau and Diefenbaker but between Drapeau's ideas and nearly everybody else's. For a time half a dozen different exhibition sites in Montreal were considered, and real-estate interests all over the city frantically lobbied the Drapeau administration. Drapeau had his own idea: enlarge Ile Ste Hélène, an island park in the St. Lawrence, and add another island (later called Ile Notre Dame).

On the face of it the idea was absurd, and it seemed absurd for a long time afterwards. New *land* for *Canada?* I remember an office joke to the effect that a Dutch engineer must have been called in by mistake. Everyone objected, from an association of birdwatchers (who said the new island would displace the mudflats nesting site of some ring-billed gulls) to the mayor of St. Lambert, a suburb on the south side of the river, who said he didn't want a Coney Island on *his* doorstep. Even after the site was finally approved, everybody at the Montreal press club knew that an engineer (no one knew who he was) had *proven* that the newly created island would sink right into the St. Lawrence. In the end, of course, Drapeau was shown to be magnificently right. Twenty-five million tons of fill were poured into the river, the islands emerged safe and sound, and water – the river itself, plus the many lagoons through the site – was one of the stars of the fair.

On August 13, 1963, when Prime Minister Pearson inaugurated the physical work of Expo by tipping 25 yards of earth onto Ile Ste Hélène, he said what was then in everybody's mind: "I would be less than frank if I did not add that I feel we all have cause for concern over the magnitude of the tasks that must be accomplished if the fair is to be the success it must be."

Twenty-five days later, the Government announced that the 67-year-old diplomat, Pierre Dupuy, Canada's ambassador to France and the most senior professional in the Canadian foreign service, had accepted appointment as Commissioner-General of Expo. Dupuy had worked with the International Bureau in Paris, had helped with the organization of the Paris Fair in 1937, and had worked on the 1942 Rome Fair (which, as it happened, never took place). From his appointment till almost the day Expo opened, Dupuy devoted most of his energy to attracting foreign countries to Expo. Somehow, by force of personality and salesmanship, by capitalizing on every friendship acquired in a lifetime of diplomacy, Dupuy compelled the world to take Expo seriously. He travelled 250,000 miles and by 1967, he had brought in sixty-two countries – the most ever to take part in a world's fair.

Behind him the Government appointed as Deputy-Commissioner a tough,

Expo's dramatic islands site was mostly man-made. Ile Notre Dame was enlarged by filling in the St. Lawrence with rubble from the excavations for Montreal's underground transit system.

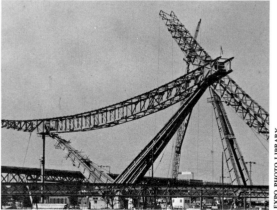

Two pavilions in the earliest stages. [*Left*] the U.S. dome and, [*above*] Russia's roof girders.

experienced businessman, Robert Shaw, till then head of the Foundation Company of Canada. Shaw became the real boss of Expo while Dupuy became its chief salesman. Shaw also brought in as director of installations Colonel Edward Churchill, who had helped General Sir Bernard Montgomery build airfields and had been the Canadian Army's construction chief.

Churchill soon became Expo's favourite legend. He introduced the strict, demanding "critical path" method to control construction, with computers to tell him each day how far behind or ahead every aspect of the construction job was. In 1963, and even 1964, everybody *knew* that a computer (no one knew whose) had forecast that Expo couldn't possibly be built in the time available. Churchill – by such blunt strategies as threatening to push somebody's pavilion into the St. Lawrence if its builders didn't maintain their schedule – managed to make it all happen.

These were the two key accomplishments at Expo – making the world take it seriously, and getting it built in an unheard-of time.

The theme of Expo was almost equally important. The fair's planners began only with the International Bureau's belief that it should be essentially non-commercial and should reflect the epoch. The theme emerged at a 1962 meeting in Montreal attended by Drapeau, Drouin, Associate Defense Minister Pierre Sevigny, and several others. Someone – Sevigny believes it was he – suggested *Terres des Hommes*, the title of a book by Antoine de Saint-Exupéry (1900-1945), whose writings often involved meditations on the place of man in the universe. In the months that followed, Expo people often quoted Saint-Exupéry's most immediately relevant remark: "To be a man is to feel that one's own stone contributes to building the edifice of the world."

At a conference of intellectuals – scientists, educators, artists – at Montebello, Quebec, the following year, the theme was refined and expanded. What emerged from the Montebello Conference was a series of theme ideas that sounded portentous and dull in the abstract but proved to be exceptionally lively in execution – Man the Explorer, Man the Creator, Man the Producer, Man in the Community. Each was to be a theme pavilion, or a complex of pavilions. Man the Creator, for instance, became a hugely successful art gallery, a world photo show, a design exhibit, a sculpture garden, and a world festival of the performing arts.

*Terres des Hommes*, translated as Man and His World, became the theme not only for Expo's own contributions but for parts of dozens of the national pavilions. It became the intellectual core of perhaps the best world's fair ever, certainly the best of our time. The people who made Expo set out with a heaven-storming ambition. They wanted to make not a good world's fair but a great one; and they succeeded. This book is about what they made and how they made it.

*Like a crystal sun, the U.S. dome rises above the man-made island.*

# Tomorrow's World

The jewel lights of Russia's palace of glass dance in the water as a gondola cruises the island canals.

*A boatered visitor appears to dance a nifty figure across the facade of the ultra-mod Venezuela Pavilion.*

*The make-believe forest of the Pulp and Paper Building was probably the fair's most photographed symbol.*

*La   Ronde the smell of patates frites. You could ride a camel or a hollow log.*

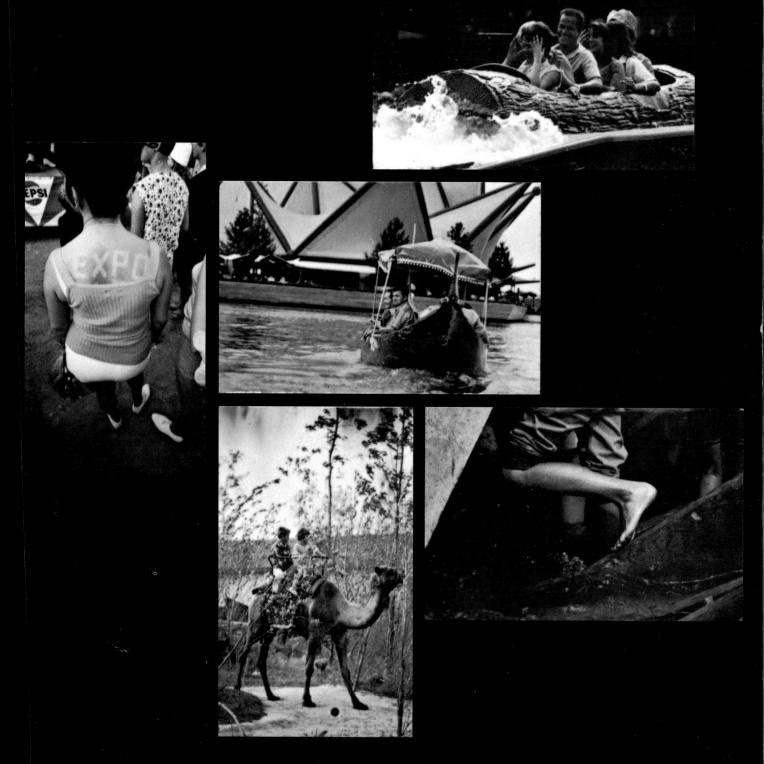

*Inside Kaleidoscope, many mirrors reflected one image to infinity.*
*Outside, the photographer finds a mirror of even greater subtlety.*

# 1 | The greatest show on earth

In the long summer of Expo, Canadians savoured for the first time the enormous pleasure of seeing the whole world take an interest in them. The Toronto *Globe and Mail* ran an eight-column headline: IMPACT OF EXPO; EVERY-ONE IN PARIS IS TALKING ABOUT IT. The Ottawa *Citizen* headed a dispatch from London: EXPO – IT'S A SOLID HIT IN THE U.K. Canadians read it, every word of it, with a kind of glee.

The reason for this was rooted in Canadians' peculiar relationship to the mass media. It is possible that Canadians now read more foreign magazines and see more foreign television shows per capita than any other people in the world. The news-stands are flooded with American (and, in Quebec, French) periodicals, and television stations, even the ones owned by the state, broadcast thousands of hours of foreign (mainly American) shows every year.

Canadians long ago grew accustomed to a peculiar form of cultural isolation, or maybe alienation. We long ago accepted that most of the mass culture we consumed had absolutely nothing to do with us – private-eye shows were about American private eyes, westerns were about the American West, and even political magazines were concerned with American or European politics. There have been marginal exceptions – *Time* has had a Canada section for years, but it's there to attract Canadian advertising money; *Paris Match* for a time ran some Canada news, apparently for the same reason. And all the U.S. magazines have for years occasionally published articles about "our neighbor to the north" – changed, since separatism became news, to "our troubled neighbor to the north." But we knew these were only minor items, nothing like as important as what happened in places like America, Britain and France, or even Cuba. We knew that foreigners didn't think us very interesting. There was no reason why they should, of course.

Then, when Expo opened, suddenly things changed. China, for instance, had previously shown concern only for the quality and quantity of Canadian wheat, but now it took the trouble actually to sneer. Expo, said the Peking

"You're right. They are Canadian geese."

"I don't know. Maybe he bounced a check at Expo."

*People's Daily* in August, was just a capitalist front. "Western monopoly capitalistic groups, headed by the United States, peddle their goods, fight for markets and expand their economic aggression." Even if this was just another excuse to knock the Russians – who had proven themselves "renegades fawning on U.S. imperialism" by taking part in Expo – it was kind of heart-warming just the same.

In Russia itself Expo became a running subject of public comment and discussion. The newspapers pointed out frequently, and piously, that the "serious" Russian pavilion was far superior to the "frivolous" American bubble. Yuri Zhukov, writing in *Pravda* in June, focussed on the issue of international competition: "International expositions are not such simple things. They are not only international shows of achievements of mankind but also sharp ideological struggles. Our Soviet pavilion in all its essence, in all its contents, is actively taking part in this struggle."

A month later Zhukov wrote again on Expo, this time about its theme and theme pavilions, seeing a sinister conspiracy behind them: "The organizers of the exposition knew that visitors to Expo would have profound thoughts about the development of today's society. They resorted to a ruse that would propel such thoughts along a less dangerous path." The ruse, Zhukov said, was in the implication, behind many of the theme pavilions, that the answer to the contrast between wealth and poverty lay in man's more efficient use of his power and knowledge. Whereas, every good Communist knew it lay in revolution.

Like many foreign journalists, Zhukov found at Expo what he wanted to find. Australian papers praised the Australian pavilion, British papers

(for the most part) the British pavilion. France's pavilion was praised in France, and Belgium's in Belgium. (This approach was not, incidentally, confined to foreigners – the Toronto *Star* at one point ran a front-page story pointing out the enormous superiority of Ontario's pavilion over Quebec's.)

In Britain some of the highbrow papers – the *New Statesman*, the *Spectator* and *New Society* among them – found serious faults in Expo (a writer for the *Spectator* thought it old-hat), but the dailies and the big magazines were wildly enthusiastic.

The *Illustrated London News* ran a special section on Canada, centred on Expo, and so did the London *Observer*. Jonathan Aitken in the London *Evening Standard* was close to hysteria: "There has never been any other show of its kind that has come near it." (Was he, one wondered, at Paris 1900 or London 1851?) The Lancashire *Evening Post* called it "the greatest man-made show on earth" and the Liverpool *Daily Post* "this year's greatest show on earth." (That same phrase, incidentally, appeared in the Launceston *Examiner*, of Tasmania.) The London *Observer* noticed quite early what some in Canada were just beginning to suspect, or hope – that Expo was changing Canada's image: "Expo 67 isn't just a world fair, it has a glitter, sex appeal, and it's given impact and meaning to a word that had neither: Canadian."

You had to be a pretty cool Canadian to read those words without a certain pleasure. A Canadian journalist, Don McGillivray, of the Southam News Services, noticed a subtle change in the attitude of the British press: "Most press and broadcast comments have been devoid of cloying sentimentality about the Commonwealth connection. Canada is being judged as an adult nation, not as a semi-dependent 'daughter country' which must be praised extravagantly for her successes and excused her failings."

The *Times* of London was still capable of a certain unwelcome motherliness – "In Britain there is pride and rejoicing in Canada's success" – but most papers were willing to see Canada as what it had, in fact, become: a friendly, related, but very separate, country.

Elsewhere in Europe, the press comment was equally enthusiastic. *Scala*, the Frankfurt magazine, called Expo "a magnificent birthday party" located on "a Canadian Venice." The daily *Helsingin Sanomat* of Finland, like *Pravda*, concentrated on the fair's relation to the Cold War: "True to their habit as competitors in the great power struggle, the United States and the Soviet Union have extended their competition in the conquest of space and the publicizing of their achievements in space to Expo 67. . ."

In Belgium, *La Chronique Industrielle*, a glossy business magazine, devoted a special supplement to Expo and contributed one of the few careful comparisons of Expo 67 and Brussels 58, the last official world's fair. Expo, said *La Chronique*, was *plus intelligente*, while Brussels was *plus charmante*.

In places like Czechoslovakia, which prepared long and lovingly for its hugely successful pavilion, Canada became something more than a place that produced wheat and hockey players. In France, Jean Creiser wrote in *Le Figaro* that by the time of Expo's closing it would have to be recognized that Canada "has attained adulthood . . . and must be taken into account on the world's map." A Canadian in Paris, speaking to Alan Harvey of the *Globe and Mail*, reported with a kind of wonderment on the new attitudes of the French people he knew: "I think what impresses them more than anything else is the fact that Montreal is exploding in a way that is neither French nor American. It has come into its own at last, and is realizing its real significance." *Paris Match*, which came out with almost the same cover picture as *Life* (a minirail vanishing into the American pavilion) declared that at Expo, for once, it was not technique that dominated but Man.

It seemed almost everybody, everywhere, was saying just what Expo's planners had hoped they would say. But, in the end, what mattered most, inside Canada at least, was the response of Americans. Suddenly something important was happening up there in Canada, and the American newspapers and magazines and TV shows were full of it. Expo's greatest boosters, in the end, were all Americans. When a critical article appeared in an American publication – like Mordecai Richler's in the *New York Review*, which called Expo "a good-taste Disneyland" – it usually turned out to have been written by a Canadian.

For once, Canadians saw themselves on American television. Ed Sullivan did a show from Expo, and Perry Como did a show about Canada. Edwin Newman of N.B.C. put together an hour-long documentary, *Expo Observed*, which charmingly and affectionately surveyed the whole fair. Radio and TV stations all over the United States – many of them the same stations to which Canadians habitually tuned – gave daily reports on Expo. One radio station, in Washington, D.C., broadcasted the temperature at Expo every morning along with its regular weather reports.

*Time* magazine – the parent *Time*, not the Canadian offshoot – called Expo "the most successful world's fair in history." *Life* reported: "In all ways, Expo, which cost $1 billion, turns out to be the biggest show ever." *Look* published an article asking, "What's Got Into Our Good Gray Neighbors?" The trade journals – architecture, engineering, film – were full of Expo. *Life* ran three major articles and the *Saturday Evening Post* two. In the second *Post* article, Anne Chamberlain ended with a paragraph that summed up the combination of amusement and enchantment so many Americans experienced at Expo:

"As I sit here now, listening to the sound-track music of *Bridge on the River Kwai* from the Beer Pavilion across the canal, a fellow in a striped shirt has just spun by in a motorized gondola, and I can see a sampan and a vaporetto rounding the bend. The blue minirail is looping above my head, and at this hour after sunset the whole site turns into a lighted soap bubble. My horoscope, which I got for a nickel when I stood on the foot-massage machine, because no one else was standing on it, says I am passionate, tempestuous, impulsive, instinctive, vernal and meditative. . . . Because there was an empty seat here at Aux Crêpes de Chez Smitty, I am also knee-deep in Belgian waffle. I think it was about when I started wiping the whipped cream off my purse that I decided not to come back to America."

On Canada's one-hundredth birthday *The Economist* of London summed up Expo's effect on the country that made it: "The acclaim won by the show on the man-made islands in the St. Lawrence may have done more for Canadians' self-confidence than any other recent event."

Certainly this was true, but there was more to it than that. Expo managed to convey to the world some sense of the complications of Canadian life, some idea of what it is that makes Canada different from other countries. In May a reporter for *L'Express* of Paris was talking to a young Quebec separatist. The French reporter referred to the obstacles overcome in the creation of Expo. The separatist replied: "We are French, yes. But don't you see that here we are, above all, Americans? In other words, we are convinced that nothing is impossible." That remark, quoted in *L'Express*, contained a hint of what some outsiders saw at Expo but found hard to articulate.

Expo, it became clear, was in quality and style not American (like the world's fair at New York in 1964-1965); nor was it European (like the Brussels fair in 1958). It had something of each – some of the dynamism and the exciting disorder of American private enterprise, and some of the careful organization and idealism behind European government planning. It could not have existed as it did without either of these qualities, but it had something else as well – a combination only Canada could produce.

This emerged in *Le Figaro* when Jean Creiser, after suggesting that some English-speaking Canadians thought Expo mainly a Quebec performance, quoted Commissioner-General Pierre Dupuy: "If we (meaning French Canadians) were the conceivers, the English Canadians were the engineers and the builders. Without them, we would not have been able to do anything. . . "

Though it received its style and its impetus from French Canadians, and from the Quebec situation of the moment, Expo was uniquely a Canadian enterprise. In much of the press comment from around the world this fact came through, and as a result some understanding of the reality of Canada came through as well. Canada's problems and accomplishments began to seem at least marginally interesting to people all over the world. Canadians began to have a sense that they were not talking only to themselves.

But Expo was also a Montreal enterprise, and Montreal's image changed perhaps even more than Canada's. Writer after writer, drawn there by Expo, went home to praise the city's beauty and modernity and unique charm. (Reyner Banham, the brilliant architectural critic of *New Society* magazine in Britain, was cool towards Expo but ecstatic about Ste Catherine Street.) In the world's eyes Montreal changed, during only a few weeks, from a possibly quaint but certainly out-of-the-way place to a city with an exciting present and a limitless future. Almost all other great fairs had been held in places already established as important – Paris or Brussels, New York or Chicago. They had, therefore, comparatively little effect on their host cities. Expo had the most profound effect on what everybody knew and thought and felt about Montreal.

There were various ways to measure the impact of Expo itself on the rest of the world. Buckminster Fuller's domes became, almost everywhere, more popular than at any point in the past. Almost everybody in the movie business seemed to think Expo had revolutionized film. Habitat, the big housing project, helped start a world-wide debate on how people should live in cities. On a less important level, the word "Expo," created at Montreal, went into the international language as a synonym for "world's fair" – the organizers of the Osaka fair in Japan decided to call it Expo '70.

My favourite personal symbol of how things changed after Expo was a comparatively modest one: a cartoon, in the *New Yorker* magazine of November 18, 1967, in which one man in a business suit says to another man in a business suit: "You don't look like a Canadian." That was, in my opinion, a post-Expo joke. It couldn't have been made the year before. It suggested that a Canadian might somehow be different, be recognizable. It suggested that, finally, a Canadian was something to *be*.

# How the world saw the fair

The world's biggest picture magazines both found the U.S. geodesic dome irresistible as a cover subject.

Expo changed the meaning of the word "Canada." It used to conjure images of scarlet-coated Mounties always getting their man while mushing along on a dog sled, and the image grew more distorted the farther abroad you went. But Expo, the jewel in Canada's centennial crown, earned so much publicity that our national image changed. The world saw Expo as: "the modern dream" (*L'Express,* Paris); "a magnificent birthday party" (*Scala,* Frankfurt); "the grandest, flashiest, most vital show of them all" (*Illustrated London News*). Canada, the writers said, was now as progressive and exciting as tomorrow. In total, 35,416 press passes were issued.

Japan　　　　　　　　　　　　Czechoslovakia　　　　　　　　　　Germany

This American report was joshing
but otherwise mostly enthusiastic.

In Sweden, readers needed a map to find Montreal,
but Eskimos and Mounties were familiar.

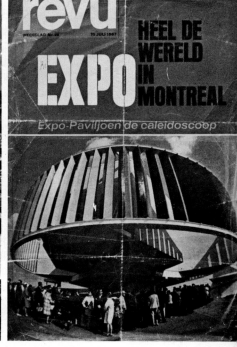

Britain  Switzerland  Netherlands

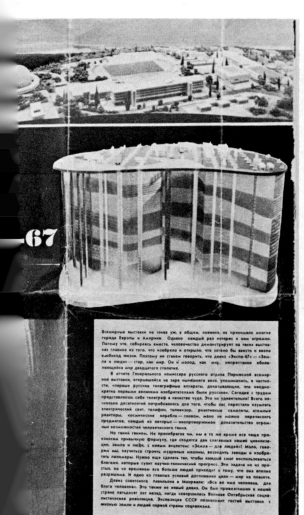

Russia's monthly *Soviet Union* featured photographs of exhibits inside the Soviet Pavilion.

France's *L'Express* posed and praised Montreal's live-wire Mayor Jean Drapeau.

Australia

Germany

Spain

Japan

Belgium

India

South Africa

# 2 | An exultation of form and structure

At Expo the walls slanted. Doors and windows were, quite often, not rectangular. Floors frequently weren't horizontal. The right angle and the straight line no longer ruled the world – there were hexagons, pentagons and truncated tetrahedrons. Not everything was made of steel and glass: there were plastics, too, and plywoods, and almost any other material you could imagine. There was so much that was fresh and different and even daring that it seemed a new world of architectural design was opening up; and some of us imagined that we might even be in at the beginning of a revolution.

Even after Expo closed, there was no sure way of telling whether this notion would hold water. In matters like architecture and aesthetics, it is hard to recognize a revolution even after it starts. World's fairs are notoriously deceptive in their effects – who could have known, for instance, that the principal influence of the Philadelphia Centennial Exposition in 1876 would be to introduce Japanese design into the mainstream of American taste? In 1851, in London, Sir Joseph Paxton was a revolutionary; but he didn't know it, and neither did most of the people who went to his Crystal Palace at that first great world's fair.

The building Sir Joseph designed to hold the great London exhibition, a gigantic greenhouse covering eighteen acres, contained all the seeds of modern architecture: it was made of standardized pre-fabricated elements (put together in only ten months); and those elements were constructed of iron and glass. The public loved that building and what it contained – the first world's fair, incidentally, cleared a couple of hundred thousand pounds and remains almost the only money-maker in the history of world's fairs – but hardly anyone knew this was a turning point in history. John Ruskin, the greatest architectural critic of the time, said it was unlikely iron and glass would "ever become important elements in architectural effort" (he noted, for instance, that they weren't mentioned as such in the Bible). John Gloag, in *The English Tradition in Design*, writes: "Joseph Paxton . . . was quite unaware of the magnitude of his achievement, and never, apparently, suspected that he had invented a new technique that was to have a profound effect upon architectural design." Even when he died, fourteen years later, Sir Joseph couldn't have known that he and his palace had found a permanent place in the history of architecture.

In modern times we decide these things more quickly. Mies van der Rohe became famous all over the world within a few years after he designed the German pavilion at the international exhibition in Barcelona in 1929. This, too, was a history-making building, both an exhibition pavilion and an exhibit in itself. It presented a new conception of flowing interior space, divided only by free-standing walls of glass and other thin materials. The roof was carried on steel columns, which stood in the open. The design was cool, clean, neat – and today you can see its grandchildren in hundreds of shopping centres and thousands of private homes.

The architectural effect of a world's fair is not always progressive; sometimes, in fact, it can be reactionary. Louis Sullivan, the great Chicago architect, once declared: "The damage wrought by the World's Fair will last for half a century from its date, if not longer." He was talking about the Columbian Exposition of 1893 at Chicago, the most celebrated (till 1939) of all the world's fairs in America. The Columbian Exposition was the result of a desire to make a fair that would be a single, carefully integrated design unit. All the buildings had the same cornice height (sixty feet) and all were in the same style – Classic Revival. Their facades, though made of lath, plaster and timber, imitated the stonework of ancient Greek and Roman buildings, often as seen through recent imitations in Europe. At night, illuminated, the Columbian Exposition became The White City, a fairyland of reassuringly old-fashioned forms. It hugely impressed its visitors, and Classic Revival became a *chic* style in the Midwest – disgusting not only Sullivan but architects for two generations after.

If Expo was an event in architectural history similar to London 1851 or Barcelona 1929, or even Chicago 1893, it was an event for which many had waited a long time. Edouard Fiset, Expo's chief architect, summed it up in his quiet way when he spoke to a gathering of American architects: "There is a marked contemporary tendency of getting away from the very severe and restrained expressions that have marked the last few decades in building and environment design . . . above all there is a great need to depart from rigid forms and to achieve a more 'humanized' expression."

Those "severe and restrained expressions" were themselves, of course, the product of a design revolution – the one that began with Sullivan and others late in the 19th century and reached its highest level in the steel and glass buildings of Mies van der Rohe. Historically, this was no bad thing: architects rightly wanted to abandon the flamboyant and the grandiose in favour of an

# The past had its place

This replica of an 18th-century Buddhist shrine [*at left*] was the focus of Thailand's display.

Historic art forms [Mexico, *left*] and architectural shapes [India, *above*] were widely used.

honest expression of contemporary techniques and materials. They wanted to get down to first principles. It was Mies who said he didn't want to make "interesting" buildings; he wanted to make good ones.

Alas, his imitators soon began to fill our cities with buildings that were neither interesting nor good. Architects became the great conservatives of our culture. Unique among artists, the architect lives in a world of profound conservatism. The people who hire him are businessmen or civil servants; the people he hires are engineers and building contractors. In not one of these groups does he find a natural sympathy for individualism. Unless he's very strong, or very brave, or both, he will himself become a part of conservative society – indeed, he may become a leader of it.

This is what happened after the great wave of Mies-type design swept over the architectural schools of Europe and North America. The architects fitted this kind of design into the tight confines of business society, and businessmen welcomed it as an economical, predictable style of building. Soon nothing looked so much like one office building as another office building. The effect was to bore us all and to deprive us of a sense of place and a sense of identity. By the late 1950s you could wake up in a hotel room in the morning, look out the window, and – for all the architecture told you – you could be in Milan or Toronto or Cleveland or Dusseldorf. Architecture had found efficiency and lost everything else.

To some people, Expo looked like a way out. As one British critic phrased it, a good world's fair is a nursery, in the sense that it's both a playground where architects can lose their inhibitions and a learning place, where they can grow up by developing or discarding behaviour patterns in preparation for a more exacting world. James Acland, of the University of Toronto school of architecture, wrote of Expo:

"At long last something of the virility and sensuous delight which have been appearing here and there in Canadian architecture will have a chance to flower in the prismatic structures of this fair. Though monotonous cubes towering into our skies have threatened to destroy every vestige of amenity and delight in our cities, the wave of protest against them has now bred a moving exultation of form and structure, and a vigorous break with our traditional pinch-penny economy."

There were critics of the Expo approach. Peter Collins of McGill University's architectural school, wrote that Expo should have integrated its architecture, that "the desire for individualistic expression seems to have become . . . rabid." But this, in fact, was the point, as Fiset saw it – individualism within a context of careful site planning and with overall high standards.

But in the architectural world to which Expo addressed itself there was more at stake than individual expression. The same international style that

Integrated transport: You could go boating, walking, climbing – or take the Expo Express.

produced the boredom in our city centres had also proved ruinously expensive in apartment buildings. Everywhere in the western world a housing crisis was growing, and those architects whose social consciousness had survived their days in architectural school were thinking of finding new ways to cover more space with less materials and for less money. "Do more with less," in the words of Buckminster Fuller.

It was in the context of these two major problems that the architects of Expo went to work.

"*Space-frame*" – the phrase covers, in different ways, the most crucial architectural innovations at Expo: the Buckminster Fuller bubble for the United States (discussed in Chapter Three); the two big theme complexes, Man The Producer and Man The Explorer; the West German pavilion; and the Netherlands pavilion. This was, as one art magazine put it, the Space-Frame Fair. The phrase is both simple and complicated. It means the effort to cover large spaces cheaply and flexibly, by distributing the weight of the building over the widest possible area; it also means a variety of complex techniques involving various kinds of aluminum, plastic, and other materials.

Take the Netherlands pavilion, an engineering accomplishment of considerable importance. It's not so much a building, more a building set. The frame consists of thirty-three miles of aluminum tubing – 57,000 pieces, each three feet long. There's no welding, no riveting: the thing is put together like a Meccano set, with wrenches, and the needed space – the exhibition room – is suspended inside. The little aluminum tubes were designed by H. G. Fentiman, of Ottawa, and are called the Triodetic system. Before the Netherlands pavilion happened, they had never been used to make a building. Now, perhaps, they will be used to make many.

The architect of the Dutch pavilion, Walter Eykelenboom, of Rotterdam, is a typical member of his profession in that he knows, better than any layman, how limited architecture has become. When Eykelenboom was given this commission he determined that it should be, like the best world's fair architecture, a step forward. He wanted to experiment with a space-frame. (In the end, curiously, his pavilion looked in photographs not unlike the Crystal Palace.)

One day, just before Expo opened, Eykelenboom was sitting in the office at the Netherlands pavilion, pleased with himself. Three years before, when he started on all this, he hadn't understood all the implications of space-frame architecture. Now he saw them as endless. Buildings now grow obsolete faster and faster. For instance, many buildings change their functions in a few years. A town may require a small town hall one year and then, ten years later, a much bigger one; in certain communities, large schools may be required in one period and smaller ones in another. Sometimes things change even faster than that – Toronto took only half a dozen years to build its great City Hall, but by the time it was occupied it was already too small to hold the city's civil service. With space-frame architecture, such buildings can be made flexible. The Netherlands pavilion can be infinitely expanded; or, it can be taken down, moved to another country, and rebuilt as two or three other buildings of different shapes. The basic structure permits any number of modifications.

More than that, Eykelenboom envisioned whole space-frame communities. Your house would be set inside this enormous space-frame and would be made to your specifications. "You would buy your house from a catalogue," Eykelenboom said. "Then it would be fitted in." The home-owner would find himself perched up somewhere in the middle of a jungle gym. Perhaps a great plastic skin would be stretched over the whole construction, to protect the inside from the weather.

Eykelenboom's Canadian associate on the pavilion was a 44-year-old, Hungarian-born Montreal architect named George Eber. In the way that some men may be said to have had a good war, Eber had a good Expo. He designed the Alcan aquarium and three minor buildings and served as Canadian associate for six foreign countries – including Germany and the United States as well as the Netherlands. Thus he became a kind of expert on space-frame architecture (he suggested the Triodetic system); before Expo was over he found himself commuting to Japan to advise on space-frames for Osaka's Expo '70. "This," he said one day, gesturing around at the Netherlands pavilion, "is the future."

Eber worked with both Frei Otto, who designed the West German pavilion, and Buckminster Fuller, who designed the American. Eber, and Expo, were

Three views of Italy: [*Above*] a worm's eye view of the *avant-garde* pavilion.

From below, and at eye-level, the roof looks as if it were about to "take off."

thus involved simultaneously on two levels of the development of the space-frame. If Fuller is the grandfather of the (still to come) miracles of space-frame, Otto will likely be their father.

Otto was 41 years old when his Expo pavilion opened. He was director of the Institute for the Development of Lightweight Structures in Berlin, and he had been a guest professor at Harvard, M.I.T., Yale and Berkeley. Architects all over the world knew he was working on a plan to build a huge skin over the entire harbour at Bremerhaven, to provide consistent weather; and on another plan to cover a valley in the Alps (plastic stretching from mountain ridge to mountain ridge) as the first major experiment in community climate control; but so far his reputation was based on theories rather than buildings. For Otto, Expo was a showcase and a chance to make an experiment that was – by the standards of his vaulting imagination – fairly modest. Nevertheless, his building was the one that aroused the curiosity of other architects on the site. They admired Fuller's dome most (as many laymen did), but what they wanted to learn about was Otto's tent. It was, after all, the first thing of its kind in the world.

Typically, Otto's space-frame took a couple of years to develop and only six weeks to build. He worked out his system – a roof of steel mesh, covering a

*Chatelaine* magazine's ideal family home included a workshop for the hobbyist husband.

plastic skin suspended from eight slender steel masts, spread over an area the size of a city block – in an elaborate model in Stuttgart. The tent itself, and all its components, were fabricated in Germany.

The German building attacked the two great problems of aesthetics and costs. As to the first, it made possible a unique and beautiful interior space, an uneven, almost anarchic "roofed landscape" lit both through the translucent plastic and through odd-shaped (and quite lovely) windows in the roof; from outside it had a clear identity and shape, and at night it glowed handsomely. As to the second, cost, the pavilion's steel and plastic roof weighed only one hundred and fifty tons – one-third to one-fifth the weight of normal roofing materials. Like Habitat and some other Expo buildings, it wasn't in itself cheap; rather it suggested economic means of building for the future.

J. M. Richards, the editor of *The Architectural Review* in Britain, summed up the two issues as they related to Otto's pavilion: "Here at last he has been given the chance of displaying the advantages – spatial, economic, and aesthetic – of tensile structures . . . This is important because in my view tensile structures are only at their beginning; they are a big part of the future of architecture – one of the most fruitful ways of escaping from the rectangular box. And although the elegantly spreading tent Frei Otto has devised for Montreal is only another temporary structure, it is already being used to try out technical improvements needed to make it suitable for permanent use."

Canadian architects (aside from associates, like Eber) had one major part in space-frame architecture at Expo: the theme complexes, Man The Explorer on Ile Ste Hélène, and Man The Producer, on Ile Notre Dame. Here the firm of Affleck, Desbarats, Dimakopoulos, Lebensold and Sise created a framework of truncated tetrahedrons around the exhibition spaces inside.

The architects were faced with the need to produce, quickly, some large buildings with large areas of open space. They decided to make them out of a kind of small building blocks, in the same way the Netherlands made its pavilion out of short metal tubes. The Canadian architects chose the truncated tetrahedron shape – a four-sided triangular figure with the corners cut off; and flattened, so that it looked rather like a prism – because it would "nest" with other such blocks, larger and smaller. Thousands and thousands of these would be built up, swiftly, into the theme pavilions.

In the plastic models the architects made, and in some of the early drawings, the theme pavilions looked graceful; obviously, Affleck *Etc.* had managed to combine efficiency and style. Alas, it didn't work out that way. This time space-frame architecture, instead of taking us into the future, dragged us into the past. The trouble started when steel fabricators announced that there weren't enough welders in Canada to make all the truncated tetrahedrons the architects would need. As a result, the units had to be made by bolting. This made them weaker (uglier, too, incidentally), and *that* meant that the thousands of pieces had to be heavily braced in place. The final result was heavy and oppressive, miles and miles of thick rusted metal; visiting those pavilions was like walking under one of the less graceful bridges of the 19th century.

If Expo was architecturally exciting as a whole, and full of hope for the future, there were many parts that one could hope would have *no* effect on anything built later. The French pavilion's great aluminum fins, for instance, looked tacked-on, like the chrome on a Detroit car; a last-minute attempt to make the ensemble appear "modern." The Soviet Union broke out of its traditional monolithic style and made, with its ski-jump roof and its glass-and-aluminum walls, a gesture towards recent western architecture; but when set down just across the bridge from the U.S. dome, the "new" Soviet architecture looked as old-hat as any of the great stone monsters of the Stalin Age. The celebrated Thaw, it became apparent, had not deeply penetrated the architectural profession.

Some pavilions presented sharp and surprising contrasts between exterior and interior. The heaviness of the big theme pavilions contrasted sharply with the ingenuity and even (occasional) elegance of the exhibits inside. The great mausoleum erected by Sir Basil Spence for the British – as James Acland put it, "It points to a deep malaise in British design, that the country could be represented by a building which would have disgraced the Wembley Exhibition of 1923" – was filled with some of Expo's most delightful and imaginative films and displays. On the other hand, the West German tent, so graceful outside, was a department store of technology inside. And the Japanese building, on the exterior a graceful steel-beam structure whimsically echoing traditional Japanese wood architecture, contained nothing but a trade fair of cameras and television sets and transistor radios. The Cuban pavilion, on the other hand, was filled with heavy-handed and oppressive propaganda; but outside it was a pleasant jumble of odd angles and box-shapes, like a Cubist painting suddenly blown up in three dimensions.

Sometimes one had the feeling that in certain cases the architects and the display designers had been introduced only *after* their work was done. This was literally true in the case of John Andrews, the Toronto architect who designed Africa Place, but here it didn't harm the architecture. Andrews put together, for the various African countries, a kind of 20th-century version of a tribal village – a series of interlocking hut-like buildings with brick walls and white plastic roofs – that emerged as one of the more pleasant collections of shapes on the site. Alas, there was seldom anything inside worth seeing.

The various other non-western countries which produced their own buildings – Thailand and Formosa, to name two – came up with what one British critic rightly called "folk-art tat," altogether alien to the Expo spirit. One other building, outside any of the architectural patterns of Expo, demands to be mentioned: the pavilion of Venezuela. These three large cubes, painted in primary colours, were unrelated to space-frame architecture and had nothing of interest to say about any other important movement in design. But in their utter simplicity they were beautifully, finally, totally *there;* as one art critic remarked, the finest piece of sculpture on the site.

The New York World's Fair of 1964-1965 was architecture as show business – it looked as if half the architects in the United States had been told to execute on a grand scale the craziest notions in their heads. It was great fun, but not consequential – the relationship between that kind of architecture and "real" architecture is the relationship between dancing and walking. But at Expo, while there was a good deal of dancing, there was something else as well. Expo was architecture as sculpture and, perhaps, architecture as history. What we experienced there was not a perfect world but a *varied* world, in which new buildings for once were surprising and delightful. Dr. Karl Schwanzer, of Vienna, the designer of the Austrian pavilion, called Expo "The most exciting collection of buildings I have ever seen," and many architects who worked on the site agreed with him.

For once the professionals and the public were in accord: in June, when the Expo corporation asked a few thousand of its visitors what they liked most about the fair, the largest group replied that they liked the architecture. They went home with eyes opened and minds refreshed; and, like the architects themselves, they would from now on be less satisfied with the constricted, conservative and ultimately boring big cities left to us by the first six decades of the 20th century.

# Architecture's giant stride into tomorrow

Sturdy hexagonal frames of British Columbia fir, each one smaller than the last, made up the spire of Man In The Community Pavilion at Cité du Havre.

Urban man may be a relatively new animal on the face of the earth, but in twenty years half of humanity will live in big cities. Architects, then, have the awesome responsibility of creating a citified world which is a monument to man's soaring potential, not a prison for his spirits; an environment that stimulates, not suppresses. At Expo they took a giant stride into tomorrow using new and often experimental ideas and materials to provide a glimpse of what's to come.

# The German tent: a breakthrough in building

All the buildings were exciting; some were breathtaking, but the German Pavilion stood out from the rest as one which, in concept and materials, may revolutionize the design of exhibition halls, auditoriums and stadiums. It was a tent – a 15 story-high, undulating, multi-peaked tent of translucent plastic, strung to a light steel mesh

Thrusting upward at oblique angles and swooping down in precipitous slopes, the German tent was a spectacular sight.

and held up by gargantuan tent poles. Except where supporting "guy rope" cables were anchored in the earth, the tent's sides were open: split-level, free-standing display floors were built independently under the great plastic umbrella. The enormous, wall-less space inside prompted one critic to compare it to a Gothic cathedral.

By day the pavilion interior was aglow with sunlight trapped by the translucent plastic. *Above* – a tent peg!

The parchment-coloured vinyl skin had a four-petal flower motif [*left*] and many windows of transparent plastic.

Despite the steel mesh, the tent roof weighed only 150 tons – one-fifth the weight of conventional roofing materials.

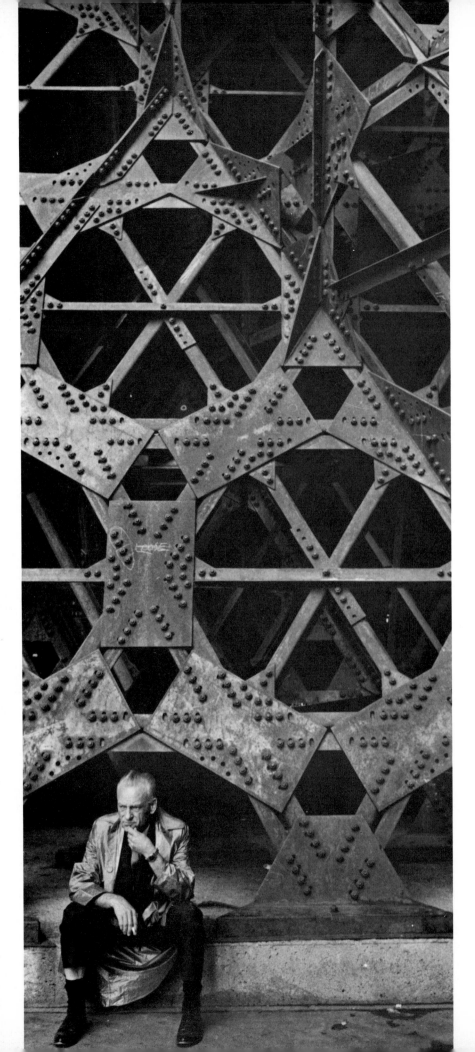

## Space frame buildings use cocoons of steel and aluminum

[*Left*] Explorer and Producer theme buildings were truncated tetrahedrons: pyramids without the points. The same shape was used in this massive trelliswork of steel, called a space frame.

[*Below*] There weren't enough welders in Canada to join the thousands of truncated tetrahedrons in the supporting frameworks, so builders used 2,500,000 nuts and bolts instead.

[*Right*] The Netherlands provided a classic space frame, in which the structural steel is built as a separate, not integral, part of the building. The walls are suspended from the frame.

[*Below*] Thirty-three miles of gleaming aluminum tubing was used in the cocoon of support for the portable three-story building. Space frame gives a structure seeming lightness.

# The harmony of an architectural symphony

If "architecture is frozen music," as one philosopher claims, then Expo was a symphony, composed by a committee of some of the world's best architects. Being largely unfettered by budgets or over-cautious clients, they produced a mind-boggling variety of design concepts and building techniques. Lacking windows, walls,

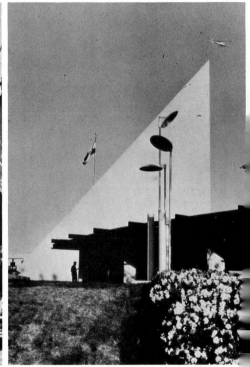

Cuba's building was cubist sculpture; India's was built around a copy of a giant 10th-century sun dial in New Delhi.

One writer said Japan built "a gigantic concrete-log cabin"; Greece's display was in white concrete blockhouses.

or a roof, some buildings were so futuristic they seemed almost freakish. Others turned to history, as with the temple or pagoda motif of some Asian pavilions. Most were just as new and exciting as their architects dared make them. The result, significantly, was harmony in this miniature city, which was at once both stimulating and restful.

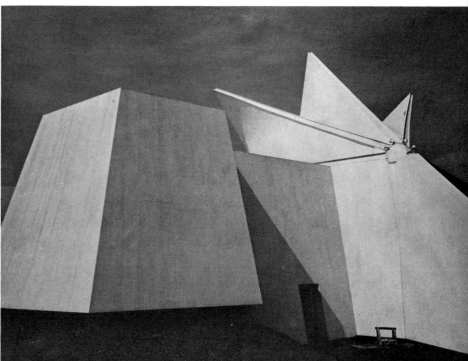

The British tower dominated this view from the French Pavilion roof; Mexico chose a star-shell of wood and aluminum.

The Western Provinces used shingles; Italy's roof was designed to seem independent of the earthbound pavilion.

Appropriately, Israel used new design and new construction techniques. The roof was geometric and the walls cubist. To create a three-dimensional crystal pattern on the walls, designers used a new fibreglass of rich texture.

# 3 | The fairest at the fair

It would have been ridiculous for the United States to demonstrate its technological supremacy in Canada, of all places. After all, United States business *owns* a large part of Canada, and in any case American technology has dominated Canadian life at least since the end of the Second World War. Nor was there any point in describing, to an audience that would be mainly North American, the nature of American life.

So the men in charge of the United States pavilion – the officials of the U.S. Information Agency – decided that this time their pavilion would charm rather than persuade, that it would entertain rather than boast. They wanted, that is, a pavilion which would express a light-hearted approach to American life, and they settled on the theme Creative America. This innocent decision led, eventually, to the most controversial pavilion at Expo – the only one, in fact, that provoked both intense praise and bitter resentment.

The U.S.I.A. people began by selecting, as the builder of their Creative America exhibit, one of the most creative Americans alive: Buckminster Fuller. He once had an idea for an apartment building that would be put in its place by a dirigible. The building would be made of lightweight alloys and the floors of it would be hung from a great mast. A dirigible would pick up the whole building and take it to where it was needed. First the dirigible would drop a bomb – that's right, a bomb – which would create a hole in the ground for the mast. Then the dirigible would put the building in place and fly away. A ground crew would pour concrete around the mast to secure it. And everybody's housing problem would be solved.

Fuller never got very far with that idea. Nor did he succeed in selling his three-wheeled automobile. And his single-family hung-from-a-mast house never worked out, either. In fact, Fuller's career for many years was a succession of well-publicized failures. In 1940, or even 1950, almost anybody could laugh at him and get away with it.

But by 1967, the year of Expo, everything was different. When Fuller arrived at Montreal for the opening of his pavilion in April he was no longer some kind of nut; he was now the grand old man of experimental design, and even some of his old detractors were willing to admit the possibility that he might even turn out to be the most influential architect of the century. Indeed, his was the most imposing creative presence on the site, and his dome – his "geodesic skybreak bubble," as he called it – was the most remarked-upon and most-admired of all the architectural accomplishments at Expo.

That was odd, since Fuller isn't officially an architect at all, certainly not a person accepted by any formal architectural society. He's an old-fashioned American inventor-type, the kind of loner who goes off into the wilderness with his own wild vision and returns with an object that is uniquely beautiful or uniquely useful or – as with Fuller's dome – both. There is something in him of Ford, and something of Edison, and something of Eric Hoffer. In fact, on the day I met him at the American pavilion, I saw him as not the architect of the place but as one of the exhibits, like the Pop Art paintings or the Indian war bonnets or the funny old election buttons – a one-man Eccentric American Inventor Exhibit.

He was seventy-one years old, a little man with a two-ear white plastic hearing aid, glasses whose lenses were as thick as the bottom of Coke bottles, and a quiet but emphatic speaking style that people might once have called "perky." Everybody who knows him calls him "Bucky," and this seems to fit. On this day he was talking, as usual, about his ideas and about the future of mankind. "Because I'm in research," he was saying, "I'm on the frontiers of man." He looked around at the fair outside, through the transparent walls of the dome. "We are all going into world man," he said. And for a moment, under the spell of his genial intensity, Expo seemed an important moment in world history and "world man" indeed a possibility. But then perhaps all moments seem important to those in Bucky Fuller's company.

He was born in 1895, in Milton, Massachusetts, of an old Yankee family, and he has made his way by an odd combination of erratic brilliance and careful Yankee shrewdness. No one, in the 1920s, would have predicted distinction for him. He was a failure in his father-in-law's construction business, a spendthrift, a hard drinker. At one point, as he tells it, he even contemplated suicide. He and his wife had lost one daughter through sickness and now they had another. At the age of thirty-two he could see no way to support his family or make anything of himself.

But in the year of the suicide impulse, 1927, Fuller's mind somehow turned around, from despair to wild ambition. At that point he developed the philosophy that has been the core of his life ever since. "I made a bargain with myself that I'd discover the principles operating in the universe and turn them over to my fellow men." Nothing less than that.

[*Opposite*] James Rosenquist's pop-painting dwarfed visitors to the U.S. art show.

Since then the ignorance of Man about himself and his world has always both intrigued and frustrated Fuller. "I have learned," he says, "that Man knows little and thinks he knows a lot. When any man can tell us just how and why he is handling and disposing the energies of his breakfast; or when any man can tell us that he is deliberately pushing each of his million head-hairs through his scalp at specifically preferred rates and in specifically controlled shapes for specific purposes, we may see that this man knows a little. But I don't know of any man who can tell me so little, even, as why we have hair." This is the sort of question to which Fuller's thought-processes lead him. As his friend David Cort, the journalist, wrote a few years ago, knowing Fuller is a stirring experience: "It is always moving to watch one man engaged in this gigantic and loving fight, alone, overmatched and blinking."

Fuller was studying both nature and modern design, and making himself into what he now says he is – a "comprehensive designer" and "an evolutionary strategist" (that is, one who plots the next evolutionary stage of Man). Out of his studies of nature he developed his characteristic shape, the tetrahedron, or four-sided pyramidal figure, the structural basis of his geodesic dome. Fuller noticed that in many aspects of nature – in the hen's egg, say – the weight of a structure doesn't rest on certain specific bearing elements, like posts or legs; rather, it's distributed over the whole surface. Out of this observation came the geodesic dome in which, by tension, extremely lightweight walls support huge structures.

In an architectural world dominated by traditional ideas of weight and stress, Fuller's dome at first seemed impossible. But over a long period he developed first a cult of admirers and then a cadre of supporters within government and private business. Since the 1940s his domes, or variations of them, have been used on the D.E.W. line, as portable housing for U.S. Marines, as a gigantic roundhouse at Baton Rouge, La., as U.S. exhibit buildings in various parts of the world, and even as private dwellings. (Fuller himself lives in a dome at Carbondale, Ill., where he is research professor at Southern Illinois University.) All the domes and their variations are carefully patented, and today Fuller – in the great tradition of once-scorned inventors – is getting rich; his patents bring him $200,000 a year.

His admirers regard the Expo dome as, in some ways, the finest single accomplishment of his career. Certainly it's the biggest of all his domes – two hundred feet, or twenty stories high, and two hundred and fifty feet in diameter. It is also the most complicated, with its elaborate system of retractable shading screens operated by computer to work in accordance with the sun's rays, thereby controlling heat within. (Technically, it's not *quite* perfect; in the summer of Expo it sometimes leaked during rainstorms.) Finally, it is the loveliest of all his works – exquisitely tinted, beautifully proportioned, a three-

The tempting, and tragic Marilyn Monroe had her own page in the giant Hollywood scrapbook.

quarter sphere that seems to fit its site ideally (some of the earlier domes, half-spheres, had a squat look). It is a great idea brought to fruition. Walter Eykelenboom, the Netherlands pavilion designer, summed up its effect on those who admire Fuller: "It is a masterpiece of technology, and it is beautiful to look at. But it is not designed intentionally to look beautiful – it is a piece of pure technique." Nowhere on the Expo site, in all the attempts to grab attention and all the various kinds of concocted "beauty," was there anything so compellingly lovely as this magnificent flowering of Buckminster Fuller's pure technique.

Everyone agreed Fuller's dome was great: the controversy was over what the United States put inside it. To build the interior structure and fill it with symbols of Creative America, the U.S.I.A. chose seven Boston designers, most of them Harvard professors, who work together as the Cambridge Seven. Previously they had done everything from an aquarium to package designs to short movies, and at the U.S. trade show in Moscow they had put together a highly praised exhibition of American graphic art.

The Seven approached their Expo assignment eagerly. Peter Chermayeff, a sometime book designer and film maker, said: "I wanted to give the feeling that this is a *now* country of action and experiment. We have tried to symbolize

58

Star of the U.S. space exhibit was a ~~Gemini~~ capsule, charred from atmosphere re-entry.
APOLLO

the dynamic attitude that we feel is unique with America." And Terry Rankine, a Harvard architectural professor, said: "We took very much to heart the request of Expo officials that it should not be made into a trade fair. We didn't want exhibits to say that 'our ball bearings are better than theirs.' We wanted to show the craftsmanship, inventiveness and creativity of the American people."

Their way of doing this was to exhibit used spacecraft, Elvis Presley's guitar, an Andy Warhol pop art painting, Raggedy Ann dolls, and several hundred other examples of American culture, past and present. They put these together with such style and ingenuity that they left many of us charmed and delighted: I thought on the day I first saw it that the United States had the best pavilion at the fair, and nothing I saw afterward made me change my mind. But many, many Americans felt otherwise.

Even before the fair opened, some of the pavilion officials were getting anxious. I remember a day in February when a U.S.I.A. press agent was sitting in the Expo press lounge nervously explaining that theirs wasn't to be like *other* pavilions, it was to be sort of *different*, an attempt to get across the *idea* of America. He didn't sound at all confident that the thing would work. And, as it turned out, he was right to be worried. The earliest and most prominent critic was Governor George Romney, of Michigan, who went through soon after the fair opened. "It was pretty on the outside," he reported, "but full of trivia on the inside. When you go through it on the minirail all you see is blow-up pictures of Hollywood actors and actresses. I was bitterly disappointed".

This tone of bitterness persisted through scores of printed comments from Americans, and frequently Americans at the pavilion itself would apologize for their country's failure. What was curious was that, while Americans disliked

Astronauts' artifacts: [*left*] space stroller's umbilical cord; [*above*] splash-down safety kit.

the exhibits, most non-Americans enjoyed and admired them. Thus, one American wrote to the Montreal *Gazette;* "I was shocked and disgusted by the exhibits . . . Most of it is so silly that it seems almost as though someone was trying to insult our Canadian neighbors." But the Montreal *Star*, far from being insulted, devoted a lead editorial to an expression of its hope that President Lyndon Johnson, on his visit, "enjoys the American pavilion as much as we do, not only for the shimmering, technical beauty of the geodesic dome but for the gentle, fun-poking modesty of the interior." (The President, after spending fifteen minutes in the building, offered no comment.)

Back home the newspaper letters columns were full of complaints from annoyed American tourists. "We left the pavilion in disgust," wrote a Garden City, New York, woman to the New York *Daily News.* "What a shame and disgrace to the United States!" wrote a reader of the Philadelphia *Bulletin.* "What a great pity that our great and glorious country should be demeaned by such a shoddy show!" wrote Mrs. Herman Busch, of Mahopac, New York, to the New York *Times.* Some American newspapers and magazines admired the pavilion (*Time, Life*, the New York *Times*) but many others didn't. The *Sun* of Springfield, Ohio, wanted to know: "Why can't we turn out a respectable image of ourselves?" A writer for the Long Island *Newsday* declared: "The interior is a sterile disaster." One back-country southern paper said Expo was a victory for Bolshevism, since the Soviets beat the U.S., and a Binghamton, New York, paper said the culture exhibited in the U.S. pavilion was a "blatant victory of the homosexual" – meaning, presumably, the "camp" and "pop" items. The saner reaction was summed up by the Washington *Star:*

"The net effect . . . is one of gawky self-consciousness. The disproportionate emphasis placed on huge blow-ups of ageing film sirens . . . can tend only to reaffirm the shopworn cliche once cherished by all foreigners – that American culture is composed of movies and chewing gum."

All these comments made it plainer than ever that, for a country's image, a world's fair can be crucial. It also made it clear that Americans did not see themselves as others saw them. The *Frankfurter Allegemeine Zietung* thought the pavilion showed "wit, elegance and irony . . . a masterpiece of intelligent wit and most pleasing self-irony." The Oslo *Aftenposten* declared: "It is completely unsolemn . . . It is literally like a breath from another world." The *Helsinkin Sanomat* of Finland said: "The U.S. pavilion communicates . . . that Americans no longer feel the need to demonstrate that their country is a great industrial power, thus they can confidently give their imagination free rein." But perhaps wit, irony and imagination are not what all of us look for in the pavilion that represents us on the world scene. Certainly many Americans are by now quite certain that at a national pavilion at a world's fair, jokes are in bad taste.

The space programme was no joke, of course, and the space exhibit was the most immediately effective of all the displays at the pavilion. Fuller's dome was an excellent place to display a certain kind of art, and a fine place for a Hollywood exhibit; but above all it was a superb place for a space show. One had the sense – after ascending the world's longest free-span escalator, 123 feet – that the geodesic dome would never have a more poetic purpose than this. You could imagine, if you cared to, that you were *in* outer space – around you was Expo, and the City of Montreal was just over that way, but if you looked directly up through the transparent acrylic bubble you could place yourself beyond the atmosphere.

The best part of the show was the collection of space vehicles suspended from the top of the dome frame. There above you was the Apollo programme's scorched 11,000-pound Command Module, the one actually launched into space in 1966, supported by three enormous (63 feet in diameter) Mercury parachutes. There was Ranger VII, the one that went to the moon in 1964, and Mariner IV, the one that went near Mars in 1965, both in full-scale models. At Expo one never quite escaped from this space show. As you left it and went through the rest of the pavilion it remained as a presence, glimpsed frequently through open spaces in the free-form interior design of the building. And when you left the U.S. pavilion it was still there, a collection of shadowy shapes you could never quite elude.

Like the dome itself, the space show provoked no hostility, only admiration. But the reactions to the rest of the contents exposed an interesting fragmentation of the consciousness of Americans. The appreciation of American mass culture can be broken down into three levels: lowbrow, highbrow, and middlebrow. The lowbrow accepts mass culture without thinking; the high-brow, these days, tends to accept it with a certain ironic appreciation; and the middlebrow tends to reject it, or even be ashamed of it. The Cambridge Seven took the highbrow approach, and that's where the trouble started. For it seems to be a fact that those people who go to world's fairs, and then express themselves on the subject, tend to be middlebrow. And when the Cambridge Seven set out to appreciate, even celebrate, those very qualities in American life which middlebrows deplore, the result was certain to be conflict.

The section devoted to The American Spirit was – in my view – stylish and light-hearted. There was a section of bird decoys, those wooden objects originally carved to attract wild fowl from the air, but which, properly appreciated, can be seen as art objects in themselves. There were *santos* (wooden sculptures of saints carved by Spanish American peasants), Indian adornments (Navajo gold bracelets, Pueblo necklaces), and dolls (including the "Columbian Exposition Rag Doll" of 1893). There were American hats representing regions and occupations, and a wooden baseball player originally sculpted as a store-front figure, and a small Alaskan totem pole.

All of this could have been appreciated calmly in the proper context, but the Cambridge Seven went much further in its celebration of American pop culture. It showed – thereby applying the adjective "creative" to – a collection of presidential campaign advertising items, from buttons to pillow covers, from banners to cigar-bands; the whole collection amounted to a record of the American style as applied to presidential politics in the 19th century. And the Cambridge Seven went farther still: it included a collection of cowboy hard-ware – high-class spurs, stirrups, branding irons. And farther still: a collection of guitars used by folk and pop stars like Burl Ives and Elvis Presley. Imagine it! The idea of Elvis Presley as not only part of American culture but as something of which Americans have no need to be ashamed! The idea, though commonplace in some circles, still shocked many Expo visitors.

In its display of paintings the American pavilion came closer to high culture as the museums accept it, but even here it baffled or enraged many Americans. For enthusiasts of recent American painting, however, it was a never-to-be-forgotten experience, one of the great events of Expo. For the fact is that American art and the Fuller dome came together as if they had been designed for each other, as if all those painters had been waiting years for just this chance.

The Cambridge Seven assigned Alan Solomon, the former curator of the Jewish Museum in New York, to put together the art show. And they gave him a space nine stories high.

"The pictures," Solomon said, "obviously had to be large in scale, given the scale of the place, and simple enough to read easily from a great distance.

Obviously a picture of great detail would be lost." Scale and simplicity: as it happened, those two words covered a great deal that had happened recently in American art. Pictures had grown bigger and bigger, and their design – in the case of many major artists – had grown more and more simple, so that the very plain, hard-edge picture (flat surface, a few stripes or squares) was dominating a large part of the scene. Solomon went to some of the leading artists and asked them to make paintings of the appropriate size and lend them to the pavilion. He couldn't pay for them, since in many cases the cost of a single painting – modern art is often priced by size – would be in the hundreds of thousands of dollars.

The artists responded with enthusiasm. James Rosenquist made a pop art painting of a boot sliding down a firepole, 37 feet high. Helen Frankenthaler painted *Painting for Expo*, 30 feet high. Robert Indiana painted some pop art numbers, 53 feet high. Ellsworth Kelly, Barnett Newman, Allan D'Arcangelo, Andy Warhol, Kenneth Noland – they all painted for the occasion, or lent from their own collections, major works. Jim Dine's painting, 35 feet by 14 feet, was two plain panels with the lettering: "These two panels have been painted with Sherwin-Williams speed print Sher-Will-Glo. The colors are brilliant cerise and flame pink. Jim Dine, Ithaca, N.Y. 1967." It was a put-on, in its way; it was also beautiful and entirely appropriate, like the rest of the show.

In the view of many American visitors, the Hollywood exhibition was *not* appropriate. How, some of them wondered, could a self-respecting nation show an ornate brass bed with a sign saying "Debbie Reynolds slept here in *The Unsinkable Molly Brown?*" How could the United States exhibit with pride a chariot from *Ben Hur* or a Yellow Cab from some old crime movies? But for others it was a superb exercise in nostalgia, beautifully carried off. There were, for instance, those three stand-up projection booths where five-minute movies, consisting entirely of famous film clips, were shown continuously. One of them was devoted to Spectacles, another to Love Scenes, another to Great Dialogues. So you could stand there and once again watch Errol Flynn in *The Sea Hawk* shout "Over the side, men" and see all the pirates in the world come at you in a swarm; or you could watch Marlon Brando, in *On the Waterfront*, as he said to his brother, Rod Steiger: "I coulda had class. I coulda been a contender"; or you could shiver with pleasure once more at Humphrey Bogart in *Casablanca* telling his piano player to play once again the love song he shared with Ingrid Bergman, *As Time Goes By*: "If she can stand it, I can – play it."

One day – I think it was my fourth visit – I stood there enchanted again by all this and the thought occurred to me that at Expo the Americans had the distinction of being the only people who admitted to their pavilion the real contents of their daydreams.

# That great American dome

Everyone enjoyed the American Pavilion—everyone except some Americans, that is. Buckminster Fuller's great bubble soared twenty stories over Ile Ste. Hélène, dwarfing everything else in sight. Inside, gay light-hearted exhibits demonstrated the spirit, the fun, of the American pursuit of happiness. There was Op art and Pop art, Elvis Presley's guitar, Tom Mix's wooden horse and a scorched space ship. But some U.S. visitors, especially politicians, thought it all trivial. While millions were amused, Governor Romney of Michigan announced: "It's silly."

It was the movies, after all, that sold the American Dream to the world, and Hollywood took a corner to itself where Marlene Dietrich and Elizabeth Taylor glittered over lesser stars.

Getting through or across the geodesic bubble — by escalator or minirail — was fast and fun . . . much *too* fast for those who had waited for hours in the queues.

CLEVELAND AND HEND

**3**

**2**

**7**

THE SAME OLD COON

HENRY CLAY
AND
FRELINGHUYSEN

**9**

**12**

**8**

OLD
GLORY

**13**

**14**

**17**

**18**

GRANT
COLFAX

**20**

HELL
SECRETARY
DRUM CORPS

1 Election hoopla in the 1800s came in many forms. This jacket plugged for Benjamin Harrison. He won.

2 Abe Lincoln's fresh face had become stoney — as this electioneering bust attests — by his second run in 1864.

3 Western saddle of gold and silver inlay was part of a $125,000 display of parade gear from California.

4 This banner bears America's national creed: "One made out of many."

5 Elaborate jewelled harness, a companion piece to the parade saddle (fig. 3).

6 A military shako — headgear for strictly ceremonial occasions.

7 This bandanna, an 1888 campaign gimmick, features the losers, Grover Cleveland and Allen Thurman.

8 The very guitar used by Elvis (The Pelvis) Presley to record Hound Dog during the rock 'n roll era.

9 The first telegraphed election results — in 1844 — tapped out defeat for the team on this banner.

10 The shako always has a pompon. The badge identifies the military unit.

11 Bunting from the 1884 battle for the White House. Left: Republican ticket. Right: Winning Democrats.

12 A give-away campaign handkerchief, painted with Henry Clay's image.

13 A glass paperweight from the time when "Old Glory" had only thirteen stars.

14 Handkerchiefs were still being given out in 1880. This one ballyhoo'd James A. Garfield.

15 This Sioux war bonnet was made from 2,000 turkey feathers, especially for Expo.

16 Stars and stripes decorated Japanese lanterns during early election campaigns.

17 This poster of Ulysses S. Grant was featured in his second successful campaign, 1872.

18 The military shako — a different design but still bearing the familiar eagle badge.

19 Masonic fez worn by the secretary of the drum corps, Hellas Chapter.

20 This is a banner from Grant's first presidential campaign, in 1868.

21 James Blaine and John Logan, Republican candidates in 1884, used this poster — and lost.

22 America's headgear: tuque, jet pilot's helmet, and, in front, the drum major's bearskin.

23 Under the great eagle, "all are invited" to hear Col. George at an 1872 election rally.

# 4 | The future of the city

The most curious fact about Expo was that many people who found difficulty getting in to see the pavilions and the films – people, in fact, who hardly got to see *anything* – still came away happy. They were pleased just to be there. Wandering around, digging the scene, riding the minirails, was for some the greatest of Expo pleasures. Part of this, of course, resulted from the sheer exuberance of Expo itself, and from what it said to Canadians about their country. Laurier LaPierre, the rising politician, historian and television star, after looking around Expo, said: "I think we'll never be the same again. Mackenzie King is dead, the Depression is over, and thank God for that. We are a very isolated people . . . now we are discovering the world."

But behind the sense of joy one felt on the site – and saw reflected in the eyes and the attitudes of so many others – there was a more specific cause: Expo itself, exclusive of its contents, was carefully designed as a "happening" that would be exciting and stimulating. And this fact may very well tell us something important about the future of our cities.

The city is, according to received wisdom, man's greatest work of art – indeed, his *only* collective work of art. Curiously, however, and despite our vast experience, we still don't know much about building cities. There are great city-places in the world – say, for instance, St. Mark's Square, in Venice – but we can't say precisely how they happened or how, in our own terms, we can equal them. We are all of us city-planners in one way or another: when you vote for a city councillor, or decide where to buy a suit, or choose to live in this district rather than that one, you are making decisions that affect the shape of your city and your children's city. In this sense, every city is the result of several million individual decisions. But making these decisions on a rational basis, so that we can create environments that will be good to live in, remains beyond us. The computer that can put together thousands of details in order to send a couple of men into orbit around the earth still doesn't know how to orchestrate the avarice of the real-estate developer, the talent of the architect, the promises of the politician, and the needs of the citizen. Expo naturally didn't solve any of these problems, but it pointed us towards some partial solutions.

Some of the people who made Expo were, consciously, propagandists, experimenters, missionaries of good city design. They knew that a great world's fair is one that changes the world, and the part of the world they wanted to change was the modern city. Norman Hay, the chief of Expo's design division, had been a design missionary for years; he ran the National Industrial Design Council (a federal government good-design propaganda agency) in the 1950s and, more recently, he had been both a designer and a critic of design. When I talked to him, just before Expo opened, he expressed his own particular hopes for the fair: "For years and years people have been hearing about industrial design and what it can do in the city. Now I think they're going to say, 'Oh, now I see what they mean.'"

In this sense, education wasn't confined to the exhibits and the films at Expo. Education in the possibilities of city life was intentionally built into the very design of the fair. "Expo itself is a work of town planning, of conceptual design and of organization," wrote Donald F. Theall, the head of the English department at McGill University, and a specialist in communications. "As a utopia, Expo reflects the global metropolis of post-sophisticate man in which we are trying to live . . . As a utopia, and as a multi-sensory total-environment poem, Expo will perform a special function of prophecy for the coming decade."

At Expo the space belonged to the people. You could hurry, or stroll, or stand still. You could eat your lunch in a space that was clean and quiet but still not far from the action. You could just sit down and look at the other people. (Who were, as it happened, one of the great unexpected sights of the fair. It was only when I returned to Expo in drab October that I realized how important a part of the visual environment were those girls in their flashing miniskirts and orange pant suits, those boys in their brilliant shirts and jackets.) The point is, it was a place for human beings to be themselves; not a place essentially for cars, or essentially for money-making, or essentially for efficiency.

There was an openness and generosity about its design that made it a very special sort of city space. It became, as Jeremy Baker noted in the Montreal *Star*, the real though temporary city centre of Montreal. "We are going to experience strong withdrawal symptoms when the fair ends," he wrote. For the fact is that, during six months, one North American city, only one, had a single large place designed for nothing less than the glorious purpose of making people happy to be there.

Consider Expo as a city centre. First, cars were all but banished (unhappily, a few V.I.P. cars were allowed on the site, along with a few cars and trucks for essential services); pedestrians thus had the right of way and most of the space.

[*Opposite*] Even underfoot, the environment was new and now. In background, Ontario's big top.

Immediately this meant the noise level was far lower than otherwise, that the air was clean, that the streets were safe.

Second, the main transport system – the Expo Express – was free of charge, unlike the transport systems in all other city centres. And, come to think of it, why shouldn't downtown transport be free? We all have to pay for it anyway, and making it free would encourage people to abandon their cars at the edge of downtown.

Third, the other form of transport, the minirail, was exciting – and why shouldn't we have this, too, in our city centres, outdoor transport placed above the heads of pedestrians so that neither walker nor rider interferes with the other? (Furthermore, the minirail was *fun* – and there's no reason why this, too, can't be borne in mind by future transport planners in the cities.)

Fourth, Expo was clean – far cleaner than any North American city centre – simply because the people running it determined that it had to be. There is no reason why ordinary cities can't be equally vigilant.

Fifth, Expo had, despite one of the wildest collections of architectural shapes in history, a sense of visual unity. This, too, was the result of careful planning; and this, too, can be applied to the new cities we are building and the old ones we are re-building.

Norman Hay was working on the Ontario Government pavilion when the chief architect of Expo, Edouard Fiset, asked him to run the design division. Hay accepted without much enthusiasm. At that point, in 1964, Expo still wasn't highly regarded across the country, despite the most earnest efforts of Pierre Dupuy and Robert Shaw. But Hay went to work there anyway, and in the end he and his colleagues accomplished a small miracle. They developed a totally unified system of design covering everything from wastepaper baskets to signs telling you where to park your yacht. And their system turned out to be one of the real successes of Expo.

Paul Arthur and Associates won the contract to design the signs. When this happened, almost any typographical designer in Canada (and a good many abroad) could have predicted how the signs would look: chaste, cool, crisp, very masculine. For Paul Arthur, as editor and designer of *Canadian Art* magazine over a ten-year period, and as designer of scores of government and commercial books and booklets, had made his tastes plain. He liked sans-serif designs (that is, no little squiggles on the ends of the letters) and he chose, for his Expo signs, the very masculine sans-serif letter form, Univers. As a result, walking around the Expo site was at times like leafing through old copies of Arthur's *Canadian Art*. It was also remarkably pleasant.

With Hay's help, Arthur imposed a strict consistency on signs all over the site. A Standard Sign Manual went out, with statements like this one, governing

When your feet ached, you took a pedicab and let someone else get the blisters.

the Expo Arrow to be used everywhere: "The depth of the arrow head equals the cap height. The arrow head is V-shaped at an angle of 45°." And: "Name tags for Expo personnel are pins attached to narrow extruded shapes into which are inserted strips with white backgrounds on which the person's name is printed in Expo letter series A (5/32″ cap. ht.)."

Of course it never worked out quite *that* strictly. Some exhibitors came to regard Hay as a kind of eccentric nuisance, and they apparently took a perverse pleasure in violating his wishes. "That always hurt my feelings," Hay said later. "Here we had made this lovely fair for them and they didn't understand that they were making so much money out of it *because* it was lovely. A lot of them never got the point." Concessionaires frequently put up signs wildly at variance with the Arthur-Hay standards, and this menace to cool design was never entirely stamped out. At one point Hay and his helpers were going around the site with red circular stickers, putting them on signs that violated the rules and were therefore condemned to come down. At another point some bureaucrat, assuming power he didn't have, ordered two hundred and fifty signs for an Expo park area, each of them saying, bilingually, Keep Off the Grass. (Hay managed to stop that just before the first of the signs went into the ground. They were doubly wrong: the words were badly designed and, by official decree, there was no Expo grass that you had to keep off.)

Paul Arthur tried to communicate as much as possible through sign-language. A sign telling you to sit down, for instance, would show a man sitting and another man standing and a line drawn through the man standing. A no-smoking sign would consist simply of a cigarette and a pipe with lines drawn through them. No words.

One encountered these little pictographs all over Expo, and they – along with the Pop and Op art signs for things like hot dogs and souvenir stands – became a kind of signature, a part of the mood of the place. They didn't always work, of course. There was one sign, a hand held up, palm out, that I never did get right. It meant: Stop, Don't Come Through Here! But I never could get out of my head the notion that it meant: Push Here To Open Door. Some of us have trouble living in the new visual world.

And then there was the embarrassing matter of the toilet signs. Paul Arthur's original signs (a man standing at attention, a woman standing at attention) proved to be too small and too ambiguous, and within a week after opening day everybody knew something was wrong. Men were wandering into women's toilets and women into men's, and some people couldn't find either. "Before Expo opened," Hay confessed, "everybody told us that would happen. We didn't believe them. We were wrong." An Expo staff designer had to work up some new signs quickly – much bigger ones, with the man much more definitely man-looking, the woman more woman-looking. Even that wasn't enough, so the words *Toilets/Toilettes* in good, large letters were added. Thus, finally, the problem was solved.

Another issue centred on the wastebaskets. There weren't enough of them, of course, because nobody expected so many people. But, worse, they didn't *look* like wastebaskets; those elegant little triangle shapes in white, who would think of throwing a paper coffee-cup in there? So they were augmented by great round drums with a more obvious sense of purpose.

Those waste-baskets were just about the only unsuccessful item in Expo's strange art gallery of street furniture. From the beginning, Hay knew that if Expo were to serve as any kind of city-centre model it would need its own style in almost everything. He wanted to make the point that there was good reason to create, within each city or town, one design chief or design consultant with control over lamp posts, park benches, and every other public facility.

In design terms, cities promote visual chaos rather than order. There were times – maybe the period just before the industrial revolution was the last time – when this wasn't so, when everything created for public use in a city fitted everything else. But no longer. Signs, overhead wires, lamp posts – they all seem to be the work of different designers with different ideas, and they usually are.

The problem lies, first, in the speed of change in the twentieth century. In the mediaeval period, when the great walled cities were built, it was possible to develop design styles gradually, perhaps over centuries. But today things change so fast that you can destroy, re-design and re-build a fair-sized neighbourhood in a few years and there's no time to develop consistent style. Thus our cities lack the firm images that mediaeval cities (and, of course, many Georgian cities) had, the sense of visual security. We often call it "charm."

Specialization of function also helps make our environment chaotic. City design tends to fall into the hands of a variety of municipal bureaucrats, each with his own fortress to defend. There's a man, usually the traffic engineer, who worries about road signs. There's a man who worries about lighting and probably has charge of the lamp posts. There's a man, usually the parks commissioner, who worries about benches. Each has power and standards of his own, each buys from certain trusted suppliers, and each has had his job forever: you are not to interfere with him. But Expo suggests the way to handle these things is to recognize municipal design as a separate function that demands special talents. Expo suggests that you must break the chaos-producing power of the individual design decision-maker (the man who chooses with some taste as well as the man who opts for ugly) and bring these decisions under common control.

At Expo this nearly didn't happen. The early attempts at an overall design plan were discouraging.

"We wanted," Norman Hay said, "drinking fountains, lights, waste-baskets, benches and so on to relate architecturally and practically. We wanted something that would work as a system; something elegant; and something not too intrusive." The waste-baskets, after all, weren't to be the *stars* of Expo; they were to be efficient and, if possible, graceful bit players.

But nothing like this came out of the studios of the Canadian designers Hay first commissioned. The first sketches Hay saw just weren't, he decided, good enough. The process dragged on, and at one point planning fell so far behind that Colonel Edward Churchill – the heroic director of installations, who applied in this as in all matters an iron hand – told Hay that if he didn't produce some acceptable drawings within ten days, he would be instructed to go out and *buy* benches and all the rest of it, and *hire* telephone booths, and stick them all together as best he could.

For a designer this prospect was nothing short of nightmarish: a great design opportunity, maybe the best of this generation, washed down the drain. Hay looked into this abyss and then cast about desperately. An Expo architect came up with the name of one Luis Villa, a Colombian designer then working in Philadelphia. After Villa was summoned it took him less than forty-eight hours to get to Montreal, and less than a week to submit his first sketches. Within the stipulated ten days, Churchill had drawings in hand. And they were, in many ways, magnificent.

Fortunately, Villa had been thinking about just this sort of thing – unified street-furniture, city-wide plans, *systems* – for years. The idea here, as Villa saw it, was to be as unobtrusive as possible and yet give unity to the site. "At Expo,"

Flying saucers? No – only Expo's graceful streetlights. The hand [*above*] says "No entry."

he said, after it was all done, "every building is totally different, and the only way you can put them together is by planning and by reinforcing the planning with design." But not the kind of design that forces itself on the visitor. In the case of the phone booths, for instance, Villa wanted to avoid the mistake of the New York World's Fair, where the phone booths were displays in themselves. And yet in the end many an Expo visitor noticed that the modest Villa phone booths, with their curving acrylic tops, their neat steel shafts, their triangular bases, were among the most handsome sculptural objects at Expo.

Villa carried that triangle through most of his designs – the benches were wood slats resting on triangles of concrete, the planters were simple concrete triangles, the drinking fountains rested on concrete bases. Villa's masterpiece, if it was not his phone booth, was the family of lighting standards. Each light consisted of a translucent fibreglass reflector at the top of the pole and a cylinder beneath. A high intensity light beam from inside the cylinder was projected up to the reflector which spread a soft, diffused glow over a wide area. The light source, of course, was invisible, so there was no possibility of glare. At Expo one of the prettiest sights was a long row of Villa light standards beside a lake.

Curiously, Villa – like the interior designer of Quebec's cool, effective pavilion, Gustave Maeder – was given almost no publicity by either the Expo public relations department or the people who wrote millions of words about the fair. In the 1960s architects have become public figures, even heroes; but the day of the celebrity-designer is not yet upon us.

"The fact is that the streets, the city milieu, has now taken on a new importance

Fourth of seven chambers of Man In The Community was this oasis of tranquility, "The Garden."

in our society. Whether the individual buildings are good matters less than the *situation.*" This is Arthur Erickson talking. Erickson has designed some of the most beautiful architectural shapes in Canada – the Man In The Community pavilion and Simon Fraser University are the most famous – but he believes we will come to place more and more emphasis not on individual buildings but on city spaces. "At Expo what mattered was that the environmental aspects of it – the landscape, the street furniture, the graphics, the transport, all worked together. The real effects of this we won't be aware of for some years."

Another architect, Raymond Affleck – whose magnificently named firm, Affleck, Desbarats, Dimakopoulos, Lebensold and Sise, designed two major theme complexes – has already begun to notice the difference. "Now every facet of the community is affected. We have clients who come to us and refer specifically to Expo standards when they tell us what they want."

Affleck described the revelation of arriving at Expo the first day the crowds were there. "We had our nose to the grindstone for four years, and then the first day was the experience of our lives. Here they were, all these people, this was the *real* 'Happening,' not the buildings or anything else non-human. In many ways Expo is the prototype of the leisure city in the era that is quickly enveloping us, and this is the message people are getting out of it. It's a place to be, an urban scene where people behave in a wonderful way to each other. This quality of human behaviour has been the important thing. That trip on the minirail – now *that's* what urban architecture is all about: moving around, that sense of movement and surprise. That's what we should have in our cities.

"The Expo corporation and the work it produced," Affleck went on, "could be a model for the solution of the whole problem of urban renewal. Three levels of government worked together with architects, engineers and businessmen, and what they produced was not only a physical miracle of construction but also the most sophisticated kind of work."

It could be argued, of course, that this was only a special occasion, in a special country, at a special time. As Affleck said, "Canadians felt that this was their total Canadian thing. The challenge was so sharp. It was like a wartime thing. It *had* to be a success."

If all this could be accomplished for a big party like Expo, why couldn't similar miracles be worked for the *really* important places, the places where people live and work, in Canada and other countries? Why couldn't the diplomacy of men like Dupuy, the brilliance of men like Shaw, the drive of men like Churchill – why couldn't this be applied, for instance, to the housing crises that are tearing the hearts out of countries and communities all over the world?

In Canada itself Expo had one very special effect: it brought into play, in a city-like situation, the talents of a whole class of people we hardly knew existed before. Jean Boucher, the director of the Canada Council, made the point shortly before Expo ended: "Most of what man has done in this country has been ugly – but there is a sort of visual revelation dawning on us now. What people will retain of Expo is an artistic visual experience.

"For the first time, the country put to use an unbelievable number of artists and designers. I think that the country will have to go on using these people. They are here, and they have demonstrated they can make things that are beautiful and effective as well. From now on it will be more and more difficult to build things which will not be aesthetically designed."

Ron Haggart wrote in his Toronto *Star* column: "After we have all seen Expo, how can any of us, ever again, be content with the cities in which we live?" How indeed? Four months after Expo opened, Montreal announced a new preliminary plan for the city and the planners' research superintendent defined it in terms every Montrealer could by then comprehend: "What we really want to do," he said, "is to generate the same sort of feeling that we've seen at Expo – fun and pride."

Montreal's plan is intended to take some account of the awesome future of metropolitan construction in North America and Europe. We are, whether we like it or not, now embarking on a period of city-building that will dwarf anything in the history of the world. North America will have to build as much living and working space in the next few decades as in the last two centuries. Right now we don't know how to do it. Possibly Expo has helped us to learn.

It was a great place to visit; maybe, in a sense, we'll find ourselves eventually living there as well.

# Reshaping the environment

Perhaps the greatest achievement of it all was that at the most superlative world's fair in history, with monumental buildings and endlessly coiling queues, no one felt dwarfed or cowed by his surroundings, and only a few threw tantrums at being asked to wait so long. The explanation was that Expo, by meticulous design, was a happy place to be; a totally new planned environment. The men who laid out the grounds and designed the surroundings did so with artists' eyes. Everything, down to litter bins, was part of the same aesthetically pleasing, subtly functional, man-sized whole. Pavilions were sited to complement one another. Signs were clear and concise and, after the first day, comfortingly familiar. It was exciting, but also restful: nothing seemed more natural than to relax. It will, hopefully, change our cities because, after Expo, they look ugly, untidy, even uncomfortable.

# Riding the blue Minirail – a bird's-eye view of the brave new world to come

The three minirails offered the best bargain for rubberneckers. Take this ride on the blue line from Ile Notre Dame.

It swooped low to zip under the Ontario Pavilion, then out over the river and up by the French Pavilion.

From their shaded comfort, riders commiserated with the long line-up at the Czechoslovakian Pavilion.

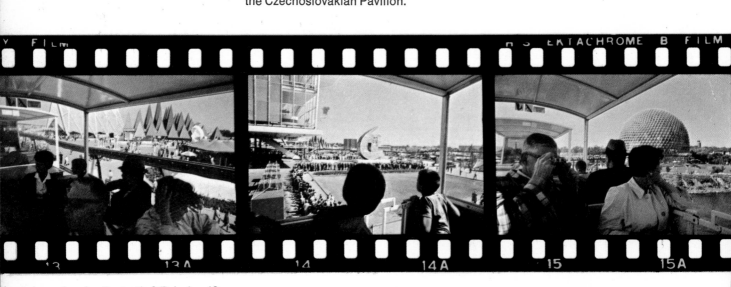

The spires of a giant's castle? Fairyland? No — a vista of the Pulp and Paper Pavilion.

this run had seats to spare, but the blue
train was so popular prospective passengers
sometimes waited for an hour or more.

Always, from canals and St. Lawrence
river, came the reminder that Man and His
World are largely water.

very new vista was exciting, but few
re so than the exotica of African and
an national pavilions.

We pass the ski-jump roof and curtain
wall of Russia's Pavilion at Cosmos Walk.

Brilliant idea! — the minirail ran
through the U.S. bubble, providing a
glimpse of the large-scale exhibits.

The ride ended on Ile Ste Hélène,
alongside Montreal Metro station, the Expo
bank and a nursery for lost children
— and adults.

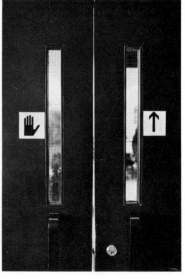

## SIGNS AS ART

The definition of a work of art has exploded until, for many, it now includes anything man-made (including soup cans) as opposed to God-given. Thus the things with which man surrounds himself must be measured with an artistic yardstick. By this token, critics said Expo itself was a work of art because it was a successful, planned Total Environment. Even the street and other official signs were, theoretically, art since they were part of the all-embracing concept designed to establish a happiness-inducing aesthetic harmony. A former editor of Canadian Art magazine, Paul Arthur, designed them.

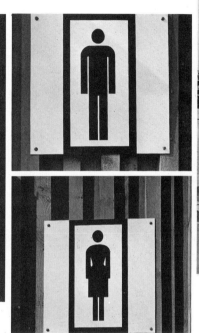

Toilette

Washrooms

In the first washroom signs [*right*] it was hard to tell boys from girls. After many blushes, they were replaced with more graphic art [*above*].

Everything was spelled out, of course, in French and English. But if you only spoke Urdu there were picture-signs as well. Those at *left* say: No smoking; No standing.

NE SORTEZ PAS LA TÊTE, LES BRAS OU LES JAMBES HORS DU VÉHICULE.

KEEP YOUR HEAD, ARMS AND FEET INSIDE THE CAR.

Minirail

← Sortie Exit Gare Station

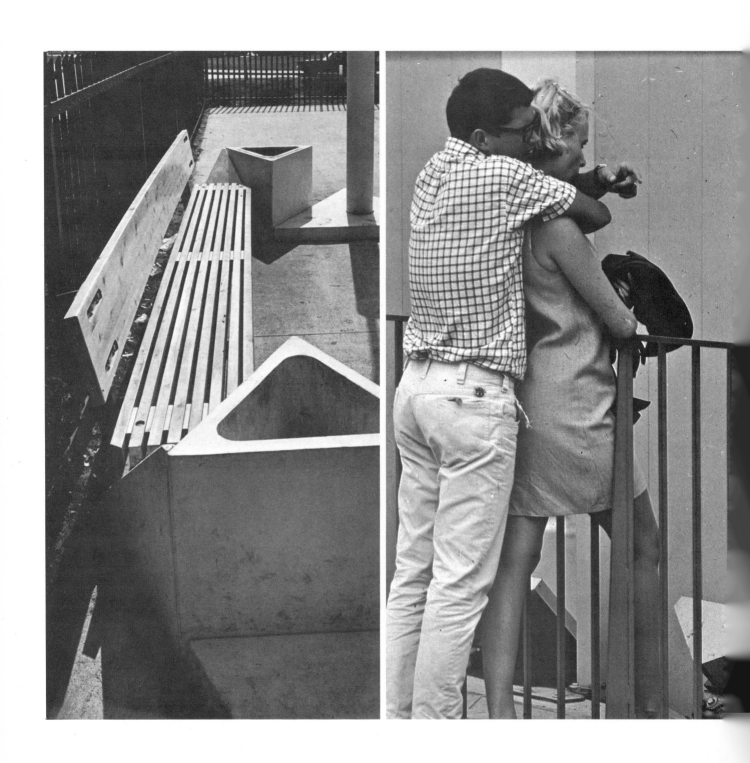

Even what town planners call street furniture was hailed as an artistic achievement. The triangular motif swept through the fairground in litter baskets, bench supports, lamp bases. Benches were gracefully linear, iron fences geometrically simple — and invitingly handy for leaning on if a man and his girl wanted to discuss the architectural advantages of pre-formed mouldings over Corbusier's curtain-wall principles. The street lights were actually elegant — and also unique, since the light itself was mounted in the top of a column and shone upwards to bounce off a circular reflector mounted atop a conventional lamp standard. And there was, perhaps, a moral to be drawn from the fact that the benches which were the city of Toronto's contribution were far more attractive, and comfortable, than those which that city provides for its own citizens.

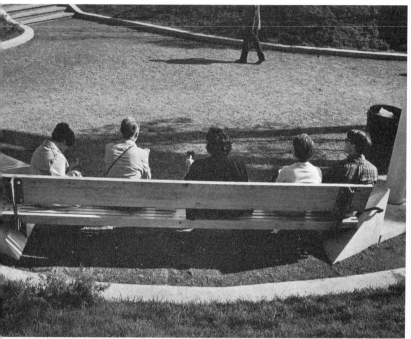

Some critics said the plastic-bubble phone booths were the most beautiful sculptures at the fair.

# 5 | A new way of seeing

To understand what happened to exposition cinema within just three years you need only compare the reaction to two films made by Francis Thompson and Alexander Hammid of the United States. For the 1964-1965 world's fair at New York, Thompson-Hammid made *To Be Alive*, the three-screen film for Johnson's Wax. It was a sensation, *the* sensation of the fair, the one thing everyone was told he must not miss: the line-ups were endless, and no one was surprised when it won Thompson-Hammid an Academy Award. At Expo 67, Thompson-Hammid were back again, this time with *We Are Young*! for C.P.R.-Cominco. Now they had six screens, and a subject everybody cared about – young people, teenagers, facing life. But *We Are Young*! was no sensation. There were line-ups, and most of those who saw it liked it, but by now the multi-screen cinema was no surprise to anyone. At Expo it was everywhere. There had been multi-screen before – not only at New York but at Brussels in 1958 and at earlier fairs, including one in Paris three decades before, and in a few isolated feature films – but this time multi-screen was a dominant factor rather than a special attraction. This time, we were present not at the introduction but at the development of a new cinematic language.

It was an exciting time. Joseph Morgenstern, the film critic of *Newsweek*, wrote: "No one who makes movies and wants to make better ones will ever be the same once he has seen the sights and smiling audiences at Expo." And Graeme Ferguson, who made the film *Polar Life*, said: "Expo will change film-making more than any other event in history."

Perhaps the real revolution was not in making films but in watching them. Expo gave us a new way of seeing, and it amounted to this: one plus one equals three. If you put two moving images side by side on the screen, the sum is greater than its parts; the eye compares and combines the two images, and the mind draws from them a fresh implication. Expo cinema forced us to look at its subjects in new ways, to stretch our visual imaginations, to *participate* in the film rather than just absorbing it.

At Expo, the cinema, as a branch of mass culture, caught up technically

with the high culture of the previous half century. What Cubism was to painting before the First World War, what T. S. Eliot's *The Wasteland* was to poetry
in the early 1920s, Expo cinema was to movies. Just as Cubism forced the viewer
to see the same object from several angles at once, and *The Wasteland* (with
its successors) forced the reader to consider various poetic images set down in
unexpected juxtaposition, so Expo cinema asked us to comprehend at the same
time two, five, seven or even fifteen separate moving pictures.

There were routine movies at Expo – hundreds of them, in fact – but those
that mattered were the multi-screen movies, and in these it was almost always
the technique rather than the content that counted. Consider the difference
between two travel-and-industry films, the one E. A. Heiniger made for Switzerland and the one Christopher Chapman made for Ontario. Heiniger's presented
the general subject of Switzerland, from mountains to chocolate factories, and
it did so beautifully. But it showed only one image – a wide image, sixty feet
by twenty-four feet, admittedly, but still only one. The film flowed freely, but
it was essentially old-fashioned; and as I left, at the end of one showing, a
woman delivered the ultimate insult: "Very educational, you know." By contrast, Chapman's film was full of intense excitement. The original pictures were
no better – if anything they were less impressive, since Ontario has no Alps –
but they were broken up, mixed up, and juxtaposed in such a way that the
effect was arresting and stimulating. Applause followed every screening.

This was true throughout Expo: multi-screen gave a sense of style and
newness to material that might otherwise have been ordinary. A mundane film
on mass communications at Man The Producer would have been textbookish
had it not been broken into four separate images. All over the site the *material*
used by the film makers was comparatively familiar, and after a while one
became used to a set of visual clichés – babies with umbilical cords, steel mills,
teenagers dancing to rock bands, cars (or motorcycles) racing down highways,
rocket-ships blasting off. But these were combined in so many different ways
that they seemed permanently fresh.

The significant shift was from one-at-a-time image-viewing to simultaneity. One could see immediately how this could be, and probably would be,
adapted to feature movies, now that the pioneers at Expo had demonstrated
the techniques. In a melodrama, for instance, simultaneity might replace traditional cross-cutting: instead of cutting back and forth between a robber
cracking a safe and a policeman coming to catch him, you could show the two
of them on the same screen at the same time. In another kind of film you could
show a character saying one thing and thinking one, two or three other things,
all at once. You could have a man talking to his boss while he thinks of his
mistress, or vice versa. One can imagine an entire film in which a worker goes
through the most depressingly monotonous routines on one screen while, on

## The delightful confusion of Laterna Magika

Laterna Magika used movies, slides, live actors, to create optical illusions and zany thrills.

There was everything from an Othello scene to shots of Prague's blonde beauties.

CZECH PAVILION

another, his mind lives a fantasy-life of dazzling variety. Once you had seen the Expo films, the new possibilities of the cinema seemed endless.

Not all the good Expo films fitted this category. The Czechs turned up with three fresh techniques all their own (see Chapter 7). The thirteen Quebec pavilion films were handsomely made, all in traditional style, and the five films in the revolving Canada pavilion theatre (including a brilliant one, *Settlement and Conflict*, by Michel Brault) were also in what we may soon be calling "monovision." *Kaleidoscope*, the three-chambered psychedelic show sponsored by six Canadian chemical companies, was outside all categories, a unique experience. Morley Markson, a Toronto designer, arranged three mirror-lined, image-filled chambers to present the theme, Man and Color. Visitors moved through the rooms, spending four minutes in each, while the filmed images around them grew more and more abstract. The mirrors produced a sensation of infinite space, abetted by the electronic music score. It was the sort of carefully programmed experience that, at any other fair, would have been a great sensation; amid the audio-visual splendours of Expo it was almost routine.

The film most people liked most – if the line-ups and my own informal opinion sampling can be trusted – was the one commissioned by the Canadian telephone companies: *Canada 67*, executed in Circle-Vision 360°, a total wrap-around process. Fifteen hundred people at a time stood in a room surrounded by movies. Nine projectors, concealed in the spaces between screens, projected a completely circular image while twelve synchronized sound channels spewed forth music and words. For some people the illusion was magical: when the cameras were up in a plane, and the plane dipped or tilted, people gasped and reached for the railings to steady themselves. When a boat was on the screen in front the audience, there was open water all around.

The content was curious. *Canada 67* was almost the only truly nationalistic film at Expo, a cinematic hymn to the glories of Canada, so blatant in its chauvinism that one could hardly imagine Canadians producing it. And, in fact, Canadians did *not* produce it: Walt Disney Studios did. *Canada 67* celebrated every Canadian symbol imaginable. It began and ended with the Royal Canadian Mounted Police musical ride (the Mounties all lined up in a circle, lances pointed, charging towards the audience from all sides). In between there was the Calgary Stampede and the Toronto Maple Leafs, the *Bluenose* and the Rockies, the Quebec Winter Carnival and the changing of the guard on Parliament Hill. In the wordy bilingual commentary, no overstatement was left unspoken. Of Canada, the narrator said: "Free men everywhere salute her centennial." At the end, *O Canada* was played. For patriots, it was a twenty-two-minute orgy.

MORLEY MARKSON

Kaleidoscope was just that: a horizonless adventure in incredible colour, motion and sound.

To make it, the Disney Studios concocted a nine-camera rig, weighing four hundred pounds. The crew mounted it on a truck and a launch, lowered it through the bomb bay of a B-25, and even managed to use it in canoes. To capture the tranquillity of a paddler in the pre-dawn mist of a northern lake, the crew lashed the equipment to three canoes and then, lying on their bellies (for the cameras pointed in *all* directions), pushed themselves slowly through the water. To some viewers, the effort seemed curiously misplaced. Depending on the range of your peripheral vision, you missed at any moment a quarter to a half of the film; it seemed to be made for people with eyes in the backs of their heads. At the same time, if you turned around to see what was happening, it usually turned out that very little was – more open water, or mountains, or whatever. Despite the wrap-around effect, there was no sense of participation. But the end of the showing produced the best applause I heard in any Expo pavilion.

The twenty-minute film in the American pavilion, *A Time to Play*, may have been less direct, but its point was more serious and its implications for future films more interesting. Art Kane, the director, set out to make a film about children's games and ended up with an overslick but effective essay on the human condition. It was overslick because the children (carefully chosen for racial balance, incidentally – a Negro here, an oriental there) were obviously rehearsed with such care that in the end their actions lacked spontaneity. But it was effective, at the same time, in conveying the intensity and earnestness with which they played their games and thus in reflecting more of the real world of childhood than most "charming" films ever do. The children played games that, again and again, prophesied the adult world – King of the Mountain, for instance, a ferociously competitive game. Kane used his three screens to convey his narrative – in Hide-and-Seek, for instance, the seeker was on one screen, a child hiding was on another. But he also used them flexibly, at times merging into one image – for a tug-of-war in one case.

Kane's effort to fabricate children's actions wasn't totally successful; if he used his screens expertly, he handled the actors awkwardly. But Francis Thompson and Alexander Hammid, in *We Are Young!*, managed both to manipulate *six* screens and to draw convincing performances from several hundred amateur actors. They began with an exuberant sequence of teenagers at play – dancing to rock bands, riding motorcycles. They showed us children riding a horse, and a couple of teenagers in a jeep racing with two boys on horses across a field. Then they followed two young girls who move to a big city to take jobs. The girls despair of the boredom of their work (one says on the soundtrack: "I wish to dictate a memo to the world at large – please accept my resignation") and some other girls take part in a peace march ("You tell us we can't change the world. We think we can.") In the end the girls, and the audience, are brought into contact with all the constructive, meaningful, non-boring work the world needs to have done; a *positive* ending.

But what mattered was the way this was done. The motorcycle sequence, for instance, involved a six-screen repetition of the image of a white line on a highway rushing furiously toward the viewer – a highly charged, uncomfortable image. The teenage dancers were shown spread across the six screens so that, simultaneously, we watched them in six different ways – a group of four in one picture, a pair in another, a medium-shot of a boy in a fourth, a close-up of a girl in a fifth. In one scene, as a girl learned how to type, we saw her puzzled face on one screen and then, around her, five close-up scenes of her hunt-and-peck typing. In another scene we watched the girls sit down to watch television, and suddenly – this was perhaps the film's most piercing moment – the six screens were filled with what they saw, the horror and banality of the world suddenly spread out before them, us, all at once.

Most of the Expo multi-screen films spread their images out horizontally. Nick and Ann Chaparos, who made *The Earth Is Man's Home*, an eleven-minute film at the Man The Explorer complex, stacked theirs vertically; their screen was thirteen feet wide and thirty feet high, sometimes divided into three equal sections, sometimes unified as one picture. It was like a Cinema-Scope screen turned on its side, but with the pictures right-side-up. Viewers sat beneath all this, in sling chairs, looking up at the film; as one critic said, it was like seeing the world through the slit opening of an astronomic observatory. The film's point was man's ability – or inability – to cope with his various environments; deserts, jungles, cities, whatever. The three screens were used

Singers and slides told the history of paper-making. The mini-dress was an added attraction.

to make didactic points, for instance, one screen showed food being scraped from a plate into a garbage can while simultaneously another showed a child in the last stages of starvation. They were also used to create mood: to show a small-town or suburban scene, the directors put a picture of a quiet street in the middle frame and flowers in top and bottom. Sometimes they showed exactly the same picture on each of the three screens, and produced a peculiarly memorable image – a repetition effect that was also used in the Ontario film. The message of the Chaparos film was vague, like Expo's – in effect, here is our world, let's do something better with it. But the film had a style and poetry that placed it among the finest cinematic accomplishments at the fair.

Most of the directors at Expo opened up the possibilities of new cinema without realizing those possibilities; they were overcome by the techniques available, and their audiences, too, went away talking about style rather than content. One exception was *Polar Life*, the film Graeme Ferguson made for showing at Man The Explorer. Ferguson triumphed not only over film technique but over a further gimmick: four slowly revolving theatres on an enormous turntable, and twelve projectors running simultaneously. Ferguson used the multi-screen technique to advantage – but he kept it in perspective: at one point a man with a tranquilizer gun shot a polar bear – the man on one screen, the bear on another. What one remembered at the end was not the turntable or the split screen but the beautiful aerial shots of icebergs off Greenland, the glimpses of life in a Siberian city with 100,000 population, the furiously excited dancing inside a community centre in some 40-below-zero Canadian town, and, above all, perhaps the most beautiful shots of the northern lights ever filmed. Ferguson, in eighteen minutes, was asked to take us inside

This well-remembered cartoon explained the interdependence of town and country.

the core of life in the polar regions, and he brought it off with consummate skill. As much as any individual at Expo, and more than most, he seemed an artist in total command of his materials.

Many of the good Expo films were exhibition cinema and nothing more; one couldn't image *The Earth is Man's Home*, for instance, being used in a movie house, without the most drastic alteration in either the film or the theatre. But even before Expo closed, one of its most celebrated films had been shown in scores of movie theatres and was scheduled for theatre showing all around the world. This was *A Place to Stand,* by Christopher Chapman, the film at the Ontario pavilion.

The difference between Chapman's film and most others was that his didn't require special equipment or a special theatre – indeed, the Ontario government was able to make a 16mm version for showing in schoolrooms. *A Place to Stand* was not multi-screen but multi-image, or "variable picture," as the people at the Ontario government called it. All the images went onto one 70mm strip of film – all ninety minutes' worth of film, crammed into a movie running seventeen and a half minutes.

*A Place to Stand* had no words, no titles; only sound effects, orchestral music, and a song ("A place to stand, a place to grow, Ontari-ari-ario"). But it had tremendous impact. It was about Ontario – industry, farming, city life, culture, sports – and the individual pictures, though not remarkable in themselves, were put together in forms that were irresistible. In one case, Chapman wanted to show a harvester working in a wheat field. He split the screen into fifteen rectangles. Fourteen of them showed only close-ups of wheat, the fifteenth a harvester advancing towards the audience. Then the rectangle containing the harvester grew and grew until it filled half the screen, wiping out the close-ups of wheat. The effect was dynamic. In another scene Chapman wanted to suggest the chaos of night life in Toronto. Here he split the screen into eight irregular hard-edged shapes, like splinters of a mirror, and filled every shape with movement and colour.

Chapman spent a year shooting his film and four months in a complex pre-editing stage that largely determined its quality. He made more than 100 layout charts indicating to the film labs in Hollywood which would do the work how each scene was to progress; in Hollywood, computers were used to translate Chapman's charts into film. In the end the Ontario government, which spent $490,000 on *A Place to Stand*, was hugely pleased. It had a film that by its sheer energy and virtuosity was changing the image of Ontario. This was cinematic propaganda on a new level.

The most important film project at Expo was a kind of a dream, or a nightmare, or maybe a secular religious ceremony: *Labyrinth*. Whatever it was, it was popular. Day after day people lined up two, three, four hours to see it; sometimes, after going through it, they would return to the line-up and tell others to stay there because it was worth waiting for. At the end of it, young people came out happy, but the middle-aged were sober. "Oh, terrific, terrific," said a little teenybopper one day when I was there. "I've never thought so hard about my age before," said a man in his fifties. Children liked it but found it confusing. Hardly anyone completely understood what it was all about.

"In a peculiar way," said Roman Kroitor, who directed it, "it doesn't really bother me that people don't completely understand. A long time ago, when we were just starting work on it, I said to the other people involved that the ideal effect would be like a very real, very vivid dream which you don't really understand. You know only that something inside it is explosive and important. The film is addressed only about twenty per cent to the ordinarily conscious part of the mind, and eighty per cent to the rest."

Kroitor and his associates at the National Film Board were assigned by Expo to produce a cinematic experience that would illustrate the theme of Man the Hero. They arrived at the idea of the labyrinth, into which, by ancient tradition, the hero would venture in order to find and kill the legendary beast at the centre. Kroitor and the others, to make the myth contemporary, developed a new kind of walk-through cinema and produced two kinds of camera mountings and went all over the world shooting film. They devised a new form of light show. They built a five-story building and filled it with three chambers. Everybody said this was the biggest event in the history of Canadian movies, but it was more than that: in the history of the world nobody had ever done anything like this before.

The hero going into the labyrinth this time was Man – the audience, everybody – and in the first chamber he was symbolized at the beginning by a baby, umbilical cord still attached. Then he became a child, climbing a construction site (the building going up one vertical screen, the ground – far below – on the horizontal screen on the floor) and then a teenager on a motorcycle and in the water. He encountered difficulties – an accident, and then a riot – in discovering that life was to be defeat as well as victory.

As the scenes faded from the two gigantic screens the visitors were led into a second chamber, a dark maze, where hundreds of tiny lights winked on and off, blinking into an infinity of mirrors, in concert with an electronic score. In the third chamber the visitors sat down before five screens arranged in a cross and here the images were concerned with the fate of the hero and his struggle with the beast – sometimes symbolic, sometimes literal. There was one magnificent five-screen scene where an Ethiopian in a dugout canoe, looking frightened but determined, paddled up to a crocodile and killed him with one violent thrust of a spear. At the moment the crocodile screamed the central screen was filled with his writhing body while the four screens around suddenly lit up with frightening still-photos of African masks: a brilliant and unforgettable use of the multi-screen process. But this last chamber was more concerned with getting across the point of Labyrinth, that the beast is not really a crocodile but something within us: as a middle-aged woman examined her no-longer-perfect face in a mirror, the voice on the soundtrack said: "The hardest place to look is inside yourself, but that is where you will find the beast, blocking your path to other men. Conquer it, and you can truly join the world."

The struggle, then, was to face oneself. But, over a scene of a European family breaking up as the young people moved to North America, the soundtrack voice said: "Just when you think you have it all, its starts to slip away." There were images of transition and death (Churchill's funeral), and towards the end the view of an ancient Angkor Wat temple overgrown by a gigantic tree. "Is the room empty or is it filled with all the shapes and sounds on earth?" In other words, do we at death join "the ground of being"– in the modern theological phrase – or do we just slip away into nothing? As the lights went up each time the faces all around the room were frozen in wonderment, caught suddenly in the act of self-examination.

Labyrinth was at once an exhilarating and a disappointing event: exhilarating because it was probably the best exhibition film ever made, disappointing because it never managed to rise above the exhibition level and become a complete work of art. There were times – too many times – when Labyrinth was interesting rather than stirring. There were moments of greatness, but these were only moments. What everyone had hoped might be an artistic experience was, instead, merely a stunning example of documentary cinema.

# Ciné Expo

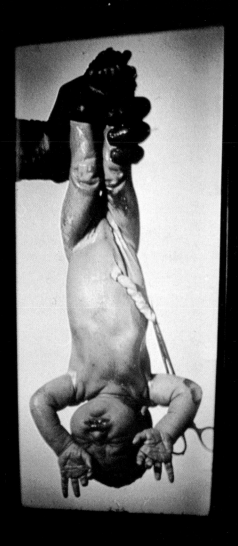

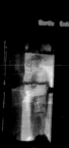

After Expo, movies may never be the same again. Nor audiences. Experimental techniques blossomed, and the two-dimensional movie vanished in a tidal wave of images designed to swamp the mind so you *feel* first, think later. In a creative explosion that blew open new doors in man's struggle to communicate with his fellows, the message was often less important than the means of conveying it. The scenes of "Earth is Man's Home" [*above*] were dramatic – but not nearly so compelling as they seemed when projected, sometimes three frames at a time, on a 30-ft. vertical screen.

A 360-degree nine-screen cocoon of Canada

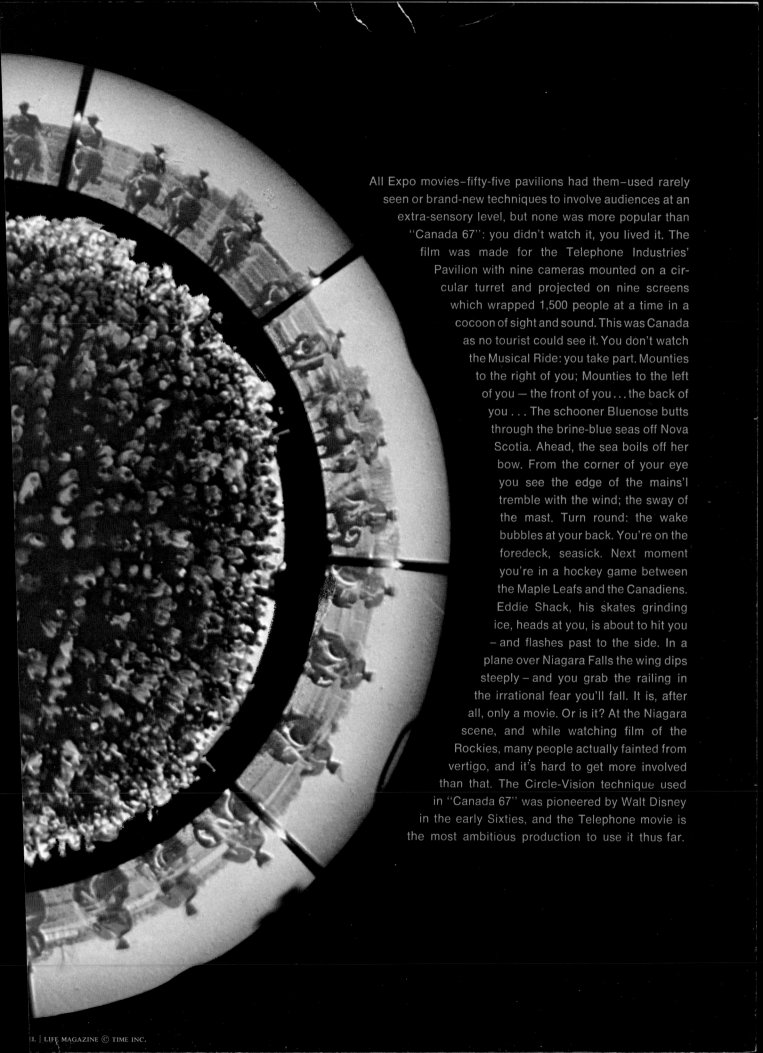

All Expo movies–fifty-five pavilions had them–used rarely
seen or brand-new techniques to involve audiences at an
extra-sensory level, but none was more popular than
"Canada 67": you didn't watch it, you lived it. The
film was made for the Telephone Industries'
Pavilion with nine cameras mounted on a circular turret and projected on nine screens
which wrapped 1,500 people at a time in a
cocoon of sight and sound. This was Canada
as no tourist could see it. You don't watch
the Musical Ride: you take part. Mounties
to the right of you; Mounties to the left
of you — the front of you . . . the back of
you . . . The schooner Bluenose butts
through the brine-blue seas off Nova
Scotia. Ahead, the sea boils off her
bow. From the corner of your eye
you see the edge of the mains'l
tremble with the wind; the sway of
the mast. Turn round: the wake
bubbles at your back. You're on the
foredeck, seasick. Next moment
you're in a hockey game between
the Maple Leafs and the Canadiens.
Eddie Shack, his skates grinding
ice, heads at you, is about to hit you
– and flashes past to the side. In a
plane over Niagara Falls the wing dips
steeply – and you grab the railing in
the irrational fear you'll fall. It is, after
all, only a movie. Or is it? At the Niagara
scene, and while watching film of the
Rockies, many people actually fainted from
vertigo, and it's hard to get more involved
than that. The Circle-Vision technique used
in "Canada 67" was pioneered by Walt Disney
in the early Sixties, and the Telephone movie is
the most ambitious production to use it thus far.

## Labyrinth

From eight balconies, visitors to the National Film Board's Labyrinth peer down at one screen, sideways at another. Images compliment or conflict – here, the screens show the victor and the vanquished.

A dramatic climax to Labyrinth's crocodile hunt: as
the spear found its mark, a piercing scream filled
the air and death masks flashed on the cruciform screen.

The U.S. movie prodded adult consciences with multi-screen demonstration of how North American children's games [*above*] reflect their parent's aggressive world.

To achieve total cinematic immersion in Man the Explorer Pavilion, the audience sat on a turntable which moved as film "Polar Life" [*below*] appeared on consecutive screens.

# A two-hour epic in 17½ minutes

 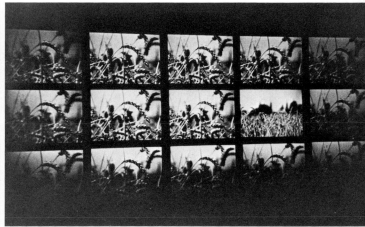

A single image like this was rare in Ontario's film. A multi-image jigsaw [*opposite page, also*] was common.

Setting scene against scene in dramatic contrast created visual excitement, made the screen leap and live.

Television shapes for a TV subject, and then a return to the wide screen for the wide open spaces.

Ontario's "A Place To Stand" was most critics' choice as the outstanding Expo film. Director-cameraman Christopher Chapman shot 35 miles of film in two years, then had it mounted, sometimes 15 images to a frame, on one 70mm master print. The result was a sometimes perplexing, frequently startling and always compelling mosaic of life, love and labour. If shown in consecutive frames, the film used in the 17½-minute movie would last two hours. As it is, the film communicates subliminally: to remember a single sequence is difficult, but having seen it you'd always have the sneaking belief that Ontario really is Eden. Of all Expo's revolutionary films, Chapman's is the only one which could be shown in neighbourhood movie houses without special equipment.

## Six screens, one message: it's fun to be young

"We are Young!" was the title; it ran in the Canadian Pacific-Cominco Pavilion. This sequence told a story of a boy and a motor cycle. He rode it from your right to your left. Then left to right. Then away from you; toward you; over you, almost. By the time it ended, you felt as if you'd ridden the bike yourself.

Expo's brilliant
film-makers never
ceased changing
or remaking the
medium. *At top,* all
six screens of
We are Young''
followed a race
over the Prairies
between a Model
T Ford and a cowpony.
The multi-image
method seems
especially suited
to the galvanic
antics of the young
set. For example,
if you suspected
the jitterbug
of being tamer than
the frug [*centre*],
your suspicion was
confirmed — sixfold.

# 6 | An argument in concrete

Reyner Banham, the British architectural critic, called it a fifth-year student's thesis that somehow managed to get built. Wolf von Eckhardt, the American architectural critic, called it possibly the first real victory of the modern industrial revolution. Perhaps Habitat 67 was both of these things. Certainly it was one of the wonders of Expo, and indeed the most explicit statement of the soaringly ambitious spirit that lay behind the entire exhibition. No institution in Canadian history had ever done anything so daring, had ever made such a costly, risky, promising thrust into the future.

In 1964, when Habitat was still only a few hundred drawings and a few dozen cardboard boxes piled on a table in a Montreal office, its architect, Moshe Safdie, explained how it was that Expo had decided to go ahead with his project. "It's the *attitude* of this fair," he said, "and that's the way it should be. World's fairs are really catalysts that accelerate the development of their time – and the more of a catalyst a fair is, the more successful it is as a fair. I think modern fairs have departed from this function of being a catalyst, but I think Expo is going back to it." Habitat was the way back, and Habitat, by the end of the fair, was the likeliest of all possible permanent symbols of Expo. What Eiffel's tower was to Paris 1889, Habitat was to Expo. The message that all those theme pavilions conveyed in elaborate films and grandiose words, Habitat said in concrete. It was, in fact, an argument in concrete – the argument of Safdie, and a whole generation of architects, that there is a fundamentally better way to make buildings for people to live in, that the masses of New Delhi and Detroit and Tokyo can be housed better and cheaper by the application of man's industrial creativity to housing. Safdie wants to bring to housing the same ingenuity-amounting-to-genius that produced, say, the modern automobile, or the cheap transistor radio. "If we built cars the way we build houses, nobody would be driving because nobody could afford it" – and Habitat is his attempt to make a revolution in how we build the places in which we live.

What Safdie demands is nothing less than the industrialization of the building process. Factory labour is more efficient than on-site labour, so why not make buildings in factories and deliver them, prefabricated, to the site? Factory work, following the assembly-line system, permits the planning of each step and the careful refining of every aspect of the process, so that the longer the process goes on, the cheaper it becomes. "What holds true for appliances, or for cars, or for aircraft holds true for houses, hospitals and schools." Repetition of the process is the key.

All of this is every-day conversation in the architectural schools, and every devotee of Buckminster Fuller knows it by heart. Architects, in fact, are now impatient with the whole idea, having come to know it so well. But in architecture, unlike some other arts, an idea remains just an idea until someone with drive, imagination and salesmanship manages to get the money and get it built. For this idea, Moshe Safdie turned out to be that someone.

He was born in Haifa, Israel, in 1938, and until the construction of Habitat began he was an architect of no serious consequence whatever. He had moved to Montreal in 1954 and studied at the McGill University School of Architecture, making it plain to everyone there that he was both a brilliant and an ambitious young man. He won an unprecedented number of prizes, and one of them was the Central Mortgage and Housing Corporation travelling fellowship. In 1959, on C.M.H.C's money, he travelled around Canada, the United States and Europe, studying the condition of housing. He was already convinced that this was the field that demanded his attention – the earliest version of Habitat was conceived, in fact, at McGill – and his travels reinforced this belief. Safdie decided that many of the world's best architects were wasting their time designing art galleries and embassies and churches – "prestige buildings" – when the masses everywhere in the world were desperate for good housing. He also decided that any sane man, viewing the results of the post-1945 building boom, must be opposed to the two main directions in contemporary residential building: 1, The single-family house in suburbia; 2, The big slab-like apartment block downtown.

1, Suburbia, he decided, simply wouldn't work anymore. The population was growing so fast (Canada, for instance, will double from 20 millions to 40 millions in this century alone) that cities were becoming intolerably large, and to continue building outwards would eventually make it necessary for a large part of the population to drive hours to work every day. Sociologists and psychologists and town planners had been worrying about suburbia for more than a decade – the adverse psychological effect of the "dormitory suburb," cut off from the reality of work, had been a favourite topic of magazine writers in the 1950s. But as Safdie saw it, the situation was beyond that, it was now reaching a critical stage. The whole idea of the city was being destroyed

MOSHE SAFDIE

This Habitat did *not* get built; it would've been five times as large as the one that did.

– people who moved there from small towns to enjoy the amenities of city life found themselves even more cut off from the excitement than they had been back home. At the same time, open country was receding. "Our cities have become a vast traffic jam. Sheer distance has made the countryside inaccessible to millions. We are simply running out of land in those areas where we most need it." Therefore, the important land, the city land, had to be used more efficiently. More people had to live on less land, so that they could be part of the city rather than spread out miles from its core.

2, But the big apartment block, while it concentrated the people on less land, was no more a solution than suburbia. Apartments lack privacy, they lack outdoor spaces; they are, almost all North Americans seem to believe, no place to bring up children. "I had a violent reaction against apartment buildings," Safdie recalled, some years after his 1959 trip, "especially those being built as public housing. It seemed mad to build structures thirty stories high, with double-loaded corridors, tiny balconies with fences around them, and inadequate space. Apartment buildings as we were building them were inadequate as family housing."

But he was convinced something had to be done, and on a massive scale. "We have to talk in terms of a million human beings at a time, and in terms of how they want to live. We cannot continue to design homes as if there were still a landed aristocracy."

This was the context in which Safdie planned Habitat. He wanted to find a way to put a great many people on a small space, and he wanted to provide them with at least some of the pleasures of private homes. He wanted to build a city into the sky, where pedestrians and cars would be separate – a 3-D city, as some planners have called it. And he wanted to make his argument graphic and convincing. He believed that town planners too often tried to sell their ideas with words alone. "It's a waste of time to talk about 3-D cities," he said, "because the public doesn't understand them. We have to supply a clear physical image that people can desire. Once they see it, if they want it, they will apply the necessary pressure on the system to make it possible." Like the people responsible for the design planning of Expo as a whole, he wanted an *exemplary* structure.

His conception of Habitat in the beginning was much grander than the structure actually erected on Cité du Havre at Expo. He proposed an arrangement five times as large: something like 1,000 apartments, with shops as well, and even a school. It was to be an experiment not in housing but in community life.

Between that point in 1964, and the start of construction in 1966, several factors stripped it down. For one thing, a tower got in the way. Habitat was to be the great symbol of Expo, but for a time Mayor Jean Drapeau of Montreal was backing a proposal to build a huge tower, on the Eiffel scale, instead. The tower was eventually abandoned, but during the time it lived in Drapeau's mind, Habitat took second place. By the time the tower faded, it was too late to rehabilitate Habitat on its original scale. So 158 dwelling units were built instead of 1,000; there were no shops, no school. What had started as a plan for a small city became instead a hugely expensive apartment building. Expo was brave; but not as brave as Safdie would have liked.

The core of Habitat was to be its construction system. Through the run of Expo a gigantic crane stood beside Habitat, a reminder of how this remarkable thing – this curious concrete mountain of dwelling places, at once strikingly modern and oddly reminiscent of primitive hill towns – had been achieved. For the point of Habitat was that its units were built on the ground and then hoisted, by the crane, up into their places five, six or even twelve stories above the ground.

First, a factory was built, beside the site Habitat was eventually to occupy. It contained four large steel moulds, in which the units were made. To make each of them, a reinforcing steel cage was first installed inside the mould. Then the concrete was poured around the cage. After the concrete was cured, hardware was installed in the shell. The unit was then moved to an assembly line. There the wooden sub-floor was installed, with electrical and mechanical services beneath it. Windows were inserted, and insulation material. Pipes

Pre-built units, including finished bathrooms, were hoisted into a child's block pattern.

were laid. Kitchens and bathrooms were installed. Finally the unit was moved to its position in the building.

There are 354 of these units in all, and the way they are put together produces the variety of forms that makes Habitat, inside and outside, so unusual. The units are arranged so as to provide fifteen different types of "houses" – you are not to call them "apartments" – up in the air. These vary from one-bedroom houses (600 square feet) to four-bedroom houses (1,700 square feet). Each has a private open garden space, 37 feet by 17 feet, each man's roof being another man's garden. Gardens in the sky are notoriously difficult to maintain – at those heights, plants tend to dry out quickly, and to die in as few as three days of heat and sun – so Habitat includes an automatic irrigation system by which water is regularly pumped to the plants.

"Habitat," says Safdie, "is your own house, your own dwelling." The arrangement of the units (plus the thickness of the walls) provides the privacy; the variation in arrangements provides for each person a sense of identity and uniqueness.

But the components, following Safdie's ideas, are rigidly standardized. The bathroom, or anyway most of it, is entirely pre-moulded in a factory on a mass-production system. Basin, tub, medicine cabinet and almost everything else – everything except the toilet, in fact – are moulded together of plastic and make a single continuous surface; so that, for instance, the wall curves out to become the edge of the bathtub and the floor curves up to become the wall and then curves again to become the ceiling. Inside one of these rooms you have a curious sense of being in another world, shut off, private; you also realize that this must be far easier to keep clean than any bathroom has ever been. The kitchen, designed in a similar way, with appliances and counters and walls all integrated, is similarly a model of efficiency. (The moulded plastic, incidentally, can be repaired. The first idea that occurs to everyone who looks inside a Habitat bathroom is that, if anyone ever cracks a surface, the whole room will have to be replaced. Not so, fortunately.)

Seen as a unit in itself, Habitat is murderously expensive. The design costs were enormous – everything had to be freshly worked out. The bathrooms cost far more than any bathroom should – "mass-production" techniques were used, theoretically, but there's really nothing "mass" about only 158 bathrooms. More important, the work was done at what Safdie estimates as 10 per cent efficiency. "We were kept at this low efficiency because we had to train workers for every job. Every operation on the project was totally new to them, and inevitably it required time for them to adapt. Because labour is half the cost of a building, this made a considerable difference in the cost of Habitat."

The engineering system chosen for Habitat added further to the cost. It was decided that, though the individual boxes would be tied together with high tensile rods and cables, they would themselves bear the weight load. This meant they had to differ in strength – the ones on the bottom being, of course, the strongest. So that as soon as the work crews had figured out how to make a box to one set of dimensions, they would be required to make a quite different one. All those boxes were not, as they looked, the same. Among some of the people who worked on Habitat there's a theory that this was a mistake, that if the idea of mass production is ever to come true, some other way should be found to bear the weight load. Safdie disagrees. He thinks that the problem can be solved in future by creating four or five different versions of the basic box, each capable of bearing a different load. This would require the most elaborate structural planning far in advance, something that was not possible with Expo's deadlines.

There were mistakes in planning, too. Only after production started – when it was too late – did Safdie and his associates notice that the units should have roofs put on them at the beginning. They had designed a box with four walls and a floor, the roof to be added later. But as the various components

There was a dazzling view from Habitat's enclosed tenth-floor pedestrian promenade.

were inserted, they were opened to the rain and snow. The contractors designed a temporary polyethylene roof, but putting it on and taking it off slowed down the work.

In the end Habitat 67 cost $22,195,920, or about $140,000 per living unit – that is, each unit cost approximately the same as six or eight ordinary town houses. If rented economically they will cost slightly more and slightly less than $1,000 a month; hardly, as it turned out, an exercise in low-cost housing.

But of course Safdie never pretended that Habitat would be economic. It was a prototype, and it proved the value of prototypes (by extension, also, the value of world's fairs, which can pay for prototypes). Because it was a prototype, zoning bylaws were changed or set aside, and the industries involved put forth special efforts. Everyone connected with the job, and the hundreds of architects and contractors who came to see it, learned about the possibility of a new approach – an approach that will replace, Safdie insists, the styles and attitudes that inhibit all serious progress in housing. At the moment, throughout most of the world, housing construction is a fragmented, specialized field. Each specialist knows little of what anyone else is doing. The architect knows nothing about the problems of the bathtub manufacturer, the union electrician works separately from the union plumber. It is as if the automobile assembly line were split up among a dozen firms, each with its own economic structure and economic demands, each with its own exclusive union. Safdie now thinks that vastly more expensive and ambitious projects are necessary, to shatter these inhibiting formulae. Habitat was just the beginning:

"The existing patterns could be broken," he says, "if we were able to pour hundreds of millions of dollars into large-scale prototypes. Unions would be forced to assume a new attitude to their role in the building industry. Private industry would become interested in bringing forth its best men and total resources. Local governments would be forced to revise dated building codes and municipal legislation. It would also force architects, engineers and contractors to recognize that the present relationship – the traditional, linear, non-overlapping approach – is as outdated as the piano roll."

Habitat thus was a prototype and – in Marshall McLuhan's terminology – a "probe" into the future. It focused attention on all the problems involved in modern housing, all the profound challenges architects, engineers and builders must face. But it also demonstrated some problems of its own. Such as:

1, *Colour:* From the beginning, people told Safdie that the dull, flat concrete-grey would look oppressive. He argued, passionately, that once the curtains were in the windows, and the plants in bloom, Habitat would come to life. He was wrong and his critics were right. The curtains didn't make enough difference to offset the boring, unfinished look of greyness. The plants, in Montreal, are there for only a few months of the year; and neither do they, even when they are there, make a serious difference. Habitat from a distance is an exciting piece of Cubist sculpture, or, depending on your taste, a handsome Pueblo village. But as you approach it, it becomes both boring and overbearing. There simply isn't enough life to it. If, in the summer of Expo, it failed to convince people that Safdie was right, and failed to make them demand new and unconventional housing-forms, then this is one of the major reasons.

2, *Pedestrian streets:* For much of the year Montreal is terribly cold, and even in late May it can often be chilly. Safdie's plastic-covered pedestrian streets, connecting the apartments with the elevators and the parking lots and the exits, are poorly sheltered from the wind. The man who lives in Habitat is much closer to the weather than anyone could wish to be; waiting for an elevator can be an ordeal.

3, *Density:* Habitat, as we saw it at Expo – in what Safdie likes to call, hopefully, its first stage – is not high-density housing. It contains about twenty units per acre, which is roughly the density of row housing. It is not economical, not even potentially economical, in the sense that an ordinary slab apartment house is; it would have to be five or six times that densely populated to compete with ordinary buildings. Here again, Safdie argues that a larger complex would have a higher density, but even a *much* larger one – with its apartment strung

## A master plan for better living

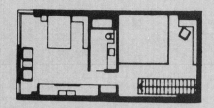

[*Left*] The basic "modular unit" — a one-bedroom apartment of 600 square feet. *Below* are some of fifteen ways to arrange two or three modules to make up houses of one or two stories, and up to four bedrooms. Patio area is roof of a lower unit. The concrete boxes are cast off-site, fitted with wooden floors, basic appliances.

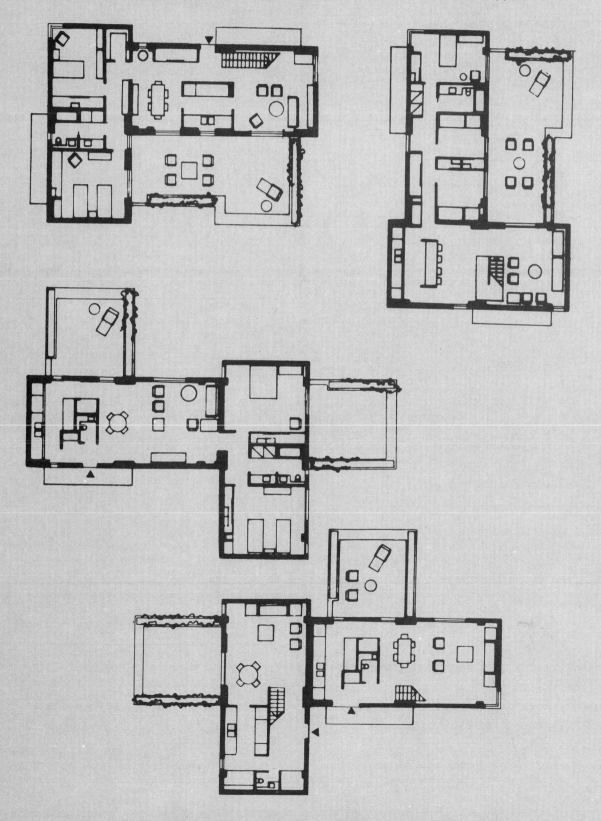

out on diagonal lines – would involve huge waste spaces inside. This is a problem Safdie will face if he continues to develop Habitat, or if he transfers the same or similar ideas to another city.

4, *The site:* Neither Safdie nor anyone else connected with Habitat could have done anything about it, but that building, as a permanent structure, is in the wrong place. Even if Expo, or part of it, becomes an annual fair, there will be little of interest on Cité du Havre during winter, at least in the near future. There may be more Habitat-style buildings later, and there will certainly be the permanent art gallery and the permanent administration building. But, as *Progressive Architecture* magazine has suggested, "When the offices at the landward end of the pier are closed, it will be a lonely, sinister walk from public transport to Habitat." Safdie has argued that Habitat will be only the beginning of a whole new waterfront development for Montreal, a re-orienting of the city towards the St. Lawrence River. But in the meantime Habitat is a building without a neighbourhood.

These are some of the things that make architects, and architectural critics, dissatisfied with Habitat. Safdie doesn't deny that it has flaws. "Habitat," he says, "is still crude, it's primitive, it's imperfect, it has a lot of problems we are still working on, but it's the beginning of a system. And, as a system, it's both a three-dimensional urban pattern and a technical building system." Looking back on Expo's decision to hire him, Safdie says: "It took courage. The established procedure for something like this, in North America particularly, is to go after a big-name architect and get the results everybody expects. People often say they want something new in architecture, when what they really want is something certified as new by the Old Guard."

Expo's courage was rewarded, beyond question. As Jean Labatut of Princeton University's architectural school put it, Habitat "is the one thing at Expo that will never be forgotten." In the constructed, heavily orthodox world of building, Habitat is a mind-expanding, stimulating event; if affects nearly everyone who sees it, even its critics.

Safdie states the problem of housing the masses in blunt, concrete terms: "The immediate problem is not how to build for less than $14 a square foot, which is the prevailing rate for multi-story housing, but how to build a better environment for $14 a square foot, and possibly, five years from now, how to build that same better environment for $8 a square foot." Towards the solution of that problem, Habitat ($70 a square foot) is only a step, but quite possibly a very important step. James Murray, the editor of *Canadian Architecture*, while severely critical of some aspects of Habitat, summed up its impact: "Habitat is a phenomenon most heartening in a nation unmarked by housing innovation since the disappearance of the wigwam . . . Housing design will never be quite the same."

# habitat

The best of world's fairs leave behind one outstanding monument, usually the embodiment of a transcendental or revolutionary idea. The fair of 1851 in England gave us the Crystal Palace, and a new understanding of the value of glass in architecture. The Paris fair of 1889 left behind the Eiffel Tower, a steel structure which influenced design for the first skyscrapers. The hallmark of Expo? It looks like being Habitat 67, a new concept of urban living which could make the city fit for people to live in once more. It uses radical ideas and building techniques to provide the convenience of downtown apartments and the spacious privacy of the suburbs, without the stifling conformity of either.

## The new city: homes and gardens high in the sky

Every window corner offers
an excitingly different
view, and no home directly
overlooks another. Most of th[e]
complex was privately rented
during the run of Expo, but 3[6]
of the units, with interior
decor and furnishings every
bit as modern as the concep[t]
itself, were open to the publi[c]

Brainchild of Montreal architect Moshe Safdie, Habitat is a 12-story complex of 158 one-to-four bedroom homes built of prefabricated 85-ton boxes hoisted into place by cranes; they support one another like blocks in a child's higgledy-piggledy pyramid. There's a pedestrian skywalk on the 10th floor level, children's playgrounds, mini-parks, and private patio gardens for each unit. When Expo ended, the homes were leased (rents up to $680) and Habitat remains as an example of what one critic called "a visionary solution to the problem of urban renewal."

The Montreal skyline, from a Habitat garden.

The washer-dryer "floats" on air.

All the rooms have concealed lighting and are air-conditioned. Built-in bookcases are a Habitat feature.

All the gay kitchens have built-in stoves, mixers and dishwashers. The "service unit" comes in one piece.

[*Left*] Bathrooms of moulded non-slip fibreglass were pre-built in factories.

[*Overleaf*] In its magnificent St. Lawrence River site, Habitat reminded world travellers of an ancient Mediterranean hillside village. Ile Notre Dame and the Katimavik appear *left,* and Victoria Bridge, *right*.

# 7 | Where the medium was the message

Czechoslovakia spent $10 million to impress the visitors to Expo. The Czechs brought a staff of three hundred to Montreal for the fair, and took over a large chunk of an apartment building to house them – they even brought their own doctor and his nurses, not out of any fear of Canadian medicine but because they figured it would be cheaper. The Czechs brought not only a pavilion, with its expensive and sumptuous restaurants and its incomparable displays, but also the elegant Koliba restaurant, down at La Ronde, in which every glass, every ashtray, was stylish; and they brought their Laterna Magika, the film-with-live-actors show. By population (Czechoslovakia has just 14 million people), the Czechs made perhaps the most ambitious single national contribution to the fair.

But then, the Czechs are exposition-prone; they enjoy exhibitions, at home and abroad, and they do them well. At Brussels in 1958 they won the gold medal for the best pavilion. The deputy commissioner-general of their Expo pavilion, Dr. Vladimir Stepanek, a veteran diplomat who is also a doctor of musicology, explained: "We like exhibitions. We are a very small country but we are a proud people. We think we have *done* something in this region of Europe where we have lived these last twelve hundred years. We have created a sort of civilization – and we want to show it, particularly to the American continent, which has not a clear idea, an image, of Czechoslovakia as a country." There was also, of course, the challenge implied by the first major fair after Brussels victory. "It was clear from the beginning, to us, that we couldn't refrain from going to Montreal," Dr. Stepanek said. "It would be considered a little cowardice."

The Czechs mounted nothing remotely resembling the pavilion most North Americans would expect from a Communist country. The art they showed, for instance, contained no hint of socialist realism, the orthodox Communist style. Czech art may have been tarnished by that brush at various points in the recent past, but not now – and not, least of all, at Expo. Here the Czechs wanted both to return to, and express, their old traditions (not denying for a moment the strength of their religious art, and the tradition it exemplifies) and to prove themselves as modern artists. They brought a wildly abstract glass sculpture that was four and a half yards high, cut from the inside in a stunning work of virtuosity, and an improbable three-ton fountain in blown glass.

A few months before Expo, Dr. Stepanek was asked about the tone of the pavilion – was it to be outspokenly Communist, for instance? He replied: "We do not conceive propaganda in these terms – big words, slogans, posters. We do not think that's good propaganda. We think the best propaganda is the truth, to show the people the true picture of a country – with all its shortcomings and good things, which you will find in a country. I think that's the best propaganda, and that's what we are trying to do in Montreal."

Art, the Czechs decided – art in all senses, from Gothic painting to new forms of cinema – is "the best propaganda." Whether it gives a precisely true picture of a country's life is open to question – certainly it was open to question in the case of the Czech pavilion, and many other Expo pavilions – but art as an instrument of state propaganda is now an established fact. A few centuries ago, art was in the service of religion, and religion, in a sense, was in the service of the government: religion established the legitimacy of kings and emperors, and gave meaning to their power. Now, in a world where formal religion means less and less, the state looks for a new form of legitimacy on the spiritual as opposed to the temporal plane. Art provides this legitimacy, or at least something more than a hint of it; the point has been recognized by politicians as diverse as John Kennedy and Josef Stalin. But art flourishes and therefore impresses only (as the Russians should long ago have discovered) in a climate of at least relative freedom. The Czech artists, since the Thaw reached Czechoslovakia a few years ago, have begun to live in such a climate.

Mr. Novak's wife has run away from him. He decides to chase her, and he enlists the help of a neighbour in his apartment building. The real reason he's chasing her is too complicated to explain, so he quickly invents a lie.

"My wife is poisoned," he says. "She swallowed some mothballs."

His neighbour first accepts this, then pauses, then asks him, curiously, "How do you know?"

Mr. Novak answers: "A strange instinct made me count the mothballs."

The neighbour accepts this as a fact.

This dialogue is not taken from a play in the tradition of the theatre-of-the-absurd, or some larky little English movie; it's part of a film that was made especially for the Czech pavilion, and it expresses – better than any description of an innovation in technique – the remarkable *style* of the pavilion.

By the time Expo was a couple of weeks old, Czechoslovakia was almost

# Wizardry in modern glass

Freed from usual Communist inflexibility, young Czechs created far-out experimental forms.

everybody's favourite pavilion. The line-ups regularly ran two or three hours, and sometimes produced congestion in the pavilions nearby. Sometimes the crush was so great that the doors had to be closed. By the end of Expo, seven million people had gone through. Of all the pavilions that counted their visitors, only two much larger and roomier ones claimed more: Russia, with 10.5 million, and the United States, with 9.25 million.

What charmed and won the people who came to the Czech pavilion was its spirit – light-hearted, gay, irreverent – and the ingenuity with which this spirit was expressed. By 1967, Laterna Magika, the brilliant Czech innovation of the 1950s, was almost routine – now it was a sideshow down at La Ronde, the amusement area, where some people found its combination of film and live actors the best entertainment on the grounds. At their pavilion proper, the Czechs now had fresh wonders to disclose – so many inventions, in fact, that it was hard for even the most dedicated pavilion visitor to take them all in. Film was the core of the pavilion, and Mr. Novak, the mothball-counter, was at the core of the most memorable of three major (there were many minor) film shows: the Kino-Automat.

Developed by a genius of cinematography named Raduz Cincera, the Kino-Automat brought to movies the governing principle of children's theatre: audience participation. Cincera reasoned that, just as children like to make Tinkerbell live by applauding at *Peter Pan*, and like to throw themselves into the action of dozens of other plays, so an adult audience might be involved in a play about adult themes. The Kino-Automat audiences – just 127 people in an intimate theatre, three times a day – took part in the action by push-button voting.

At five or more points in the plot (it varied according to what answers the audience gave), the film stopped and the audience was asked which way Mr. Novak, the hero, should act. Meanwhile, the actor playing Mr. Novak, Miroslav Hornicek, appeared in the theatre in person, and – still in character – appealed for help in solving his problems. Each viewer was asked to push either the green or the red button beside him at each decision-point. The votes were registered by seat number on a border around the screen, so that you could see your own vote counted; and a computer reported the total.

The film started with an apartment building on fire, and immediately we were told that Mr. Novak held himself responsible for starting the fire. "I'm to blame for all this," he announced. He then took us through a series of flash-backs describing the wildly unlikely but somehow logical sequence of events which had brought him to this position – how he, through carelessness, stupidity, *etc.*, had allowed a situation to develop in which a woman left her electric iron on in her apartment and thus burnt down the building. As the actor and the film told the story, Mr. Novak – and a hostess who served as master of ceremonies – allowed us to dictate some of his actions; alternate film sequences could be projected from the booth according to how we voted. But no matter what we decided, the result was the same – a burning building. Some of the Czechs responsible for showing the film said privately that it was really a sly, hidden satire on democracy: everybody gets a chance to vote, but voting never changes anything. A press release prepared by the film makers put the point much more generally: ". . . the story always returns to the same outcome. This aspect illustrates the experience of man in our modern society: life continues along the road of destiny irrespective of man's decisions." (Actually, the fire was started by an old lady who just liked being rescued; Mr. Novak had nothing to do with it, and at the end, the audience – by now completely in love with him – had the satisfaction of voting him not guilty.)

*One Man and his World* was expertly written comedy. The English dialogue (there was no French version, the Czechs having decided it was complicated enough without being bilingual as well) was excellent. At one point Mr. Novak was suspected of sleeping with a married woman. The woman's husband said that he understood, it was the woman's fault: "My wife is a sexual primitive, like some creature pounding through the jungle." But, comic quality aside, what fascinated everyone who sat through the adult Kino-Automat (there was also a version for children, with animated animals) was the quality of the audience decisions. To understand this, you need to know a little of the plot.

Mr. Novak's problems began when, just before his wife was due home, he confronted at the door of his apartment a beautiful blonde woman clad only in a towel – somehow she had locked herself outside her own apartment next door. *Question:* should he let her in? *Audience answer* (every time): Yes. Later, when his wife (misunderstanding everything, of course, as in all comedy) ran away, Mr. Novak pursued her in a car. A policeman hailed him down. *Question:* should he break the law and keep driving? *Audience answer* (nearly always): Yes. Later still, Mr. Novak believed that a young man who could help him was in a certain apartment. *Question:* should he dash in and find the young man, even though the apartment tenant tried to bar his way? *Audience answer* (nearly always): Yes. Finally, a porter barred Mr. Novak's way when he was trying to put out what looked at that point like a minor fire. *Question:* should he hit the porter over the head and go about his business? *Audience answer* (usually): Yes.

One day when I was there we voted 85-32 for admitting the blonde, 91-25 for breaking the traffic laws, 79-38 for dashing into that apartment, and 91-38 for smashing the porter over the head. That, with some variations, was how it went all through the Expo run. In the first 112 performances the audience instructed Mr. Novak to hit the porter over the head 111 times. Audiences voted always for the adventurous course, whether it was prudent or not, whether it was moral or not. Raduz Cincera summed it up: "What we are doing here really is making a sociological and psychological study about group behaviour. It is fantastic. We are learning that people decide not on a moral code but on what they like to see." Not, possibly, the most startling discovery in the history of the cinema, but certainly a remarkable statistical confirmation of what some of us had always suspected about movie audiences – not in terms of "group behaviour," as Cincera said, but in terms of what might be called "group fantasy." Kino-Automat was great entertainment, the funniest forty-five minutes at Expo; it was also a new way to study psychology.

It was altogether fitting that in the Kino-Automat the Czech pavilion should involve the fantasy lives of its visitors, because in many ways the whole pavilion was a kind of fantasy-land, a wonderland of images and objects, of glass, toys, and textiles. Even heavy industry became, in the Czech film makers' hands, a subject of fantasy. Joseph Svoboda, the distinguished stage designer, supervised the two most stunning cinematic walk-through events of the pavilion, both of them under 21st century names: Polyvision and Diopolyecran.

Polyvision presented a panorama of Czech industrial life in an eight-minute show of cinematic poetry, *Czechoslovakia – The Automated Country*. It used twenty slide projection screens, ten ordinary motion picture screens (eight front-projection, two rear-projection) and five rotating projection screens. The subjects here were all the usual things—hydro-electric power plants and textile industries and rolling mills – but they were presented in a manner that was eye-jolting and charming at once. The screens themselves were unconventional. Some were cubes onto which images were projected from outside, others were cubes with rear-projectors hidden in them, and many would move backwards and forwards, or sideways, during the show – so that the motion-picture screens were themselves in motion. There were other projection surfaces formed by steel hoops which spun around so fast that they seemed to form solid spheres – and yet they were *not* solid: one had the sense of looking at a surface while looking through it at the same time. This was accompanied by a ten-track stereophonic sound unit, and all of it was controlled by automated electronic memory circuits which switched the projectors off and on, moved the screens around, and even dimmed the lights at the appropriate moment. It was, as *American Cinematographer* magazine said, a "cinematic ballet."

Diopolyecran was, if anything, more absorbing: it gave a fresh meaning to the word "involvement" as applied to audio-visual experience. You went into this large room and sat on the rug and watched something quite new under the sun: a wall of 112 cubes which moved forwards and backwards and on which there appeared the most incredible collection of shifting, changing images. This was the result of a truly remarkable work of design engineering. Each of those two-foot cubes contained two Kodak Carousel-S slide projectors which projected still photos onto the front of the cubes.

The Zamecka [it means "Castle"] was the most luxurious of the four Czech restaurants.

In all there were 15,000 slides involved, in an eleven-minute show. The boxes could move to three separate positions, within a twenty-four-inch range, so that taken together they had the effect of a flat surface turning into a three-dimensional sculpture and then turning into a flat surface again. To run this elaborate show, the Czechs invented a memory centre with 240 miles of circuitry which changed the slides and moved the cubes automatically and registered an error the second any cube moved out of a synchronization with the others. In the course of each show the memory system, coded onto a filmstrip, issued 756,000 separate instructions.

The material to which the Diopolyecran was dedicated was nothing less than *The Creation of the World of Man*. On the 112-part screen, the earth came awake, flowers bloomed, tigers suddenly appeared, the first men walked the earth, machinery was invented. Sometimes the sequences amounted to lessons in abstract art—a girl's face would appear complete at one moment and then, at the next, be broken up in a composition suggestive of Picasso. As with so many experiments at Expo, the Diopolyecran material suggested even more than it delivered. It could hardly be classified as fine art; and, as communication, it was vague enough to mean something different to everyone in the room. But as pure technique it was a stunning experience. One wanted to see it used again, often, by artists who could realize its dynamic potential.

The sign beside one exhibit said: "Two humble men from the country spent 40 years working on the most beautiful object they could for children." And there it was, a piece of folk art that in itself made the Czech pavilion's Children's World section a very special place. It was the Trebechovice Bethlehem, a biblical tableau with 300 mechanically operated moving figures and 300 static ones, created late in the 19th century by two Bohemian farmers with artistic ambitions and a wild idea. Elsewhere there were Jiri Trnka's fairytale puppet theatre and art created by Czech children. The total effect was both relaxed and magical, but that Bethlehem tableau stood as a kind of symbol of all the non-cinematic exhibits at the pavilion: they were dedicated, most of them, to the twin ideas of tradition and craftsmanship.

The glass exhibit, for instance, ranged from 9th-century costume jewellery to elaborate contemporary pieces created for Expo. The sculpture went back to the Vestonice Venus (an eight-inch figure in baked clay that may be 25,000 years old) and included statues from the 12th century. There were Gothic paintings never before shown outside Czechoslovakia, and Bohemian coins four centuries old. No other country, except France, brought so many treasures to Expo; and, according to the stories, no other country had so much opposition from local art curators who were fearful of what might happen when chunks of the national heritage were carted several thousand miles away. (In the end, no harm was done – there was little vandalism at Expo, and the Czechs were victims of none of it.) But then, as one official of the pavilion told an American reporter: "We are not a large or important country. We are not often on the world's front pages. And when we get a chance like this, we do our best."

Their best was very good. The Czech pavilion was as close to a perfect example of display technique – seen as an art on its own – as Expo offered us. The building itself was functional rather than distinguished: a fairly plain, sedate building, designed, after a national competition, by a 37-year-old architect named Miroslav Repa. But inside, everything was surprising, and every surprise was carefully programmed.

In each place the "information cascade" offered to the viewer was calculated to fit inside the average person's attention-span (eight minutes is ideal for a film show, the Czechs think) and areas of heavy information content were alternated with quiet or even nearly empty areas. In each scene presented to the visitor, the individual elements – architectural setting, film, photographs, lettering, solid objects – were drawn together as one unit, with each bit carefully placed. In all cases pictures were assumed to be far more important than words, and things to see as far more important than things to hear. In the Czechs' hands, at Expo, the display pavilion was obviously turning into a science as well as an art, and there were designers on the Czech team who could explain

Ancient statues of twelfth-century monarchs who reigned over the kingdoms which are now Czechoslovakia stood brooding in the Hall of the Centuries.

One reason why the Czech Pavilion was the surprise success of the fair: the terrace was gay with far-out figures in ceramics.

such things as the relative value of visual impact (four-fifths) and aural impact (one-fifth) in a picture-and-sound show. Listening to them, and examining their work, you had the sense that the Czechs made a very great many of the other display artists at Expo look like rank amateurs.

The walk-through process was precisely organized – you never *wandered* at the Czech pavilion, just as you would never wander around a concert hall during the performance of a symphony. The entrance was carefully planned (the restaurants to one side, adding a note of graciousness, and then the open spaces welcoming the visitor at the front door); and the art works on the ground floor were just numerous enough to be engaging but not numerous enough to be baffling. One way, however, the programming didn't work: because of the great queues outside, too many people were allowed in; so that sometimes the crowd around an interesting object resembled a mob.

In a forty-page outline of their pavilion, issued before it opened, the Czechs said: "The predominant features are . . . the humanistic and democratic trends which finally led to socialism in Czechoslovakia." (Stalin, presumably, had nothing to do with it.) But this message was never conveyed obviously – a few words near the entrance, to the effect that Czechoslovakia was a humanistic culture under Communism; nothing more. The Russians overwhelmed their visitors with a titanic show of technological power and a few thousand words about the status of women, health services, and so on. The Czechs made their point with subtlety. One of the pavilion officials, when asked why, for instance, there was no major exhibition of machinery, replied: "People want to get away from over-civilization, from the stress of daily life, from machines. People are longing after beauty. The people of North America are no longer impressed by industrial achievements. They take them for granted. They're even oppressed by them." So there was to be nothing oppressive in the pavilion of Czechoslovakia. There was also to be nothing jarring, and nothing to hint at, say, any difficulties between the generations in Czechoslovakia – the rock bands that delight the teenagers of Prague weren't mentioned, nor were the rebellious long-haired teenagers themselves. Ontario might tell you that some of its young people play electric guitars, and the United States might celebrate Marlon Brando; not Czechoslovakia. They maintained throughout an elevated tone and a quasi-intellectual atmosphere.

In this case, as Marshall McLuhan puts it, the medium was the message. The medium was the pavilion itself, and the message was that a country which could produce a walk-through art object as delightful as this one must be, in some significant way, admirable. Even some of those visitors who hate and fear the very idea of Communism found themselves, perhaps against their will, thinking about Czech society in a fresh, surprised way. Possibly that was the greatest of all the Czechs' triumphs.

# The bewitching wonderland of the Czechs

Alongside the massed-tractor solemnity of the Russians and the relative earnestness of other nations, there was something intriguingly improbable about the Czechoslovak Pavilion. All that glass, for instance: glass fountains, glass pillars, glass walls, glass sculptures – glass poured and tortured into an enchanted forest of shapes that trapped the light and toyed with it until the result was almost mesmeric. Then there was the surprise that a simple display of exquisite crystal glassware could be spellbinding. Elsewhere there was a 25,000-year-old statue, a replica of Good King Wenceslas' crown, a nativity scene like no other, pretty girls in a fashion show and a movie you could direct yourself. And all this from behind the rusty old Iron Curtain: the only uncompromisingly industrial exhibits were an epicyclic gearcase and a turbine rotor – and to the uninitiated even these functional objects looked impressive modern sculptures.

**The wait was long, but the tour was always worth it**

Two hundred years ago, in a labour of love of God, two farmers in what was Bohemia and is now Czechoslovakia spent 40 years carving 2,000 figures, buildings and animals for a nativity scene which depicts life in Bethlehem at the birth of Christ. Three hundred figures move. In itself, the Trebechovice Bethlehem is an act of faith which inspires faith and, seeing it, some people weep. The Czech government, whose communism denies the existence of God, proudly explained it is worth $300,000.

[*Below*] It's all wood and it moves: Bohemian sawyers at work.

[*Below*] Each of the Wise Men had his own retinue on the way to the manger.

[*Right*] Bandsmen raised their instruments as if they were really striking up a tune.

[*Opposite*] The Czech show was a surprise success and poor planning for its 3-hour queues was one of its few flaws.

## Into the land of make believe

"Children's World" was a place you could pause and remember the time when goodness and virtue and truth always triumphed. Most of the stories illustrated were by Hans Christian Andersen, and this scene is from "The Snow Queen," one of the most famous of his stories. It tells how a girl rescues her brother from the Snow Queen's palace.

The house is enchanted and has eyes in its roof in "The Tinder Box," in which a humble soldier outsmarts a witch, then uses her magic to win the hand of the Princess. Even in Communist lands, monarchies live on in childhood fantasy.

### The puppet master

Fairy godmothers and swan-maidens and frog-princes and big bad wolves have no nationality, no politics, no one language. Children everywhere know that "Once upon a time . . . they all lived happily ever after." No child knows it better than Jiri Trnka, who is 55 years young. For enshrining fairyland in puppet and cartoon films, Czechoslovakia made Jiri a National Artist, awarded him the Order of Labour and commissioned him to design the Czech Pavilion's "Children's World," a bewitching re-creation of some of the world's best loved stories.

A little girl is lost on a remote planet, with only a robot to care for her. It tries, but robots have no love to give, so the girl weeps until, *presto!* — she's back on earth with Grandma. The name of this space-age fairy tale is "The Cybernetic Grandma."

What else could a swan be but a bewitched prince or princess? In "The Prince and the White Swan," from which this scene is taken, the bird is a beautiful Princess who doubles as a swan occasionally. The Prince sees her, falls desperately in love, and . . . well, guess the rest. Besides, it's better to be turned into a swan than a frog.

## The very old, the very new

According to the Czechs, the 14th century writings that describe this carved version of The Last Supper identify the disciples with such titles as "the drunkard" and "the glutton;" not with their more reverent biblical names. Thus no one knows which apostle is sleeping on the table. The carving was once part of a church altar.

One wall was a photograph tour of the country, but most visitors stopped to admire the brightly hued Gobelin, tapestry, of ornate baroque design. It was loomed in northern Bohemia in the late 18th century and was one of many art treasures on display which are normally kept in state museums.

[*Opposite*] Fabric as abstract art supplied a singular display of the Czech imagination. [*Far right*] The pavilion's was dotted with gay ceramic sculptures representing ghosts, animals, a girl with birds and a lady with a dog. They seemed to be placed there mainly as props for snap-happy photographers.

## Do-it-yourself movie making

The Kino-automat movie, "One Man And His World," let audiences write the plot – and be daring, vicariously. Nine times the film stopped for viewers to vote on alternative fates for the characters, who sometimes appeared on stage and screen simultaneously. Most audiences, voting with "yes-no" buttons on the arms of their seats, chose the daring – and amoral – alternatives. For instance, in the frame above, only 36 of the audience of 127 wanted the hero to obey the traffic cop. But whatever choice was made, the film always ended the same way. Fate, said Kino-automat, is inexorable: no man can change his destiny.

## A blonde in a fix

The blonde from next door is locked out. His wife is due home. Should he let the girl in?

The janitor pushes his way into the action. Should he be clubbed, asked Kino-automat?

Caught by fire, our hero is flushed into view as he saves the girl from a death worse than fate.

## The world and its creation as an unfinished jigsaw puzzle

Polyecran means multiple screens. The prefix "dia" indicates each screen has two projectors. The completed Czech diapolyecran was a mobile mural 32 by 20 feet consisting of 112 two-foot square cubes, each containing two slide projectors which provided the images. The cubes moved incessantly, in or out, sometimes all at once, but usually a few at a time. Occasionally an overall picture was recognisable [see the locomotive, *opposite, at bottom*], but usually only part of the whole was identifiable: spiders, or bearded men, or a gallery of girls. The rest was almost hallucinatory. It was a series of mammoth jigsaw puzzles with always a few pieces missing. Flipping them at the rate of five a second, the 224 projectors flashed 15,000 colour slides in 14 minutes to tell a version of "The Creation of the World": the story of how man changes raw materials into products.

**A divertissement on diversification**

Like Diapolyecran and Kino-automat, Polyvision was
unique. It was an arena 55 feet long by 20 feet high and
20 feet deep. From the ceiling, the Czechs hung everything but the kitchen sink. There were swirling orbs,
cubes, mirrors, a saxophone, even a weaving loom. Onto
this assortment were projected 8,000 colour slides and
eight short films. The visual effect was chaotic; the background music unearthly. The display was called Symphony. Its message: Czech industry is highly diversified.

# 8 | The education of actual experience

A few days before Expo officially opened, Colonel Edward Churchill, the fair's master builder, was standing beside one of the exhibits at Man And The Oceans, speaking to a group of visitors. "This," he said, gesturing at the half-completed exhibits around him, "has a tremendous educational input. You know, we have forty thousand schoolchildren a day programmed to go through." *Input? Programmed?* They were odd words, it seemed, to apply to the act of telling little children about life in the polar regions or how chemical fertilizers work or what a human cell is all about. But Colonel Churchill had it right, for this was a new world of education opening up. The 935,631 schoolchildren who were programmed at Expo in groups, and the millions of others who came with their parents or by themselves, were subjected to some very special forms of education and propaganda; so, for that matter, were the adults.

At Expo, electronic education became a fact instead of a theory. What everybody had talked about for years was suddenly *there*, suddenly made real. The theme pavilions – $40 million worth of them – and some of the national pavilions managed to turn education on its head. Learning became a pleasure rather than a chore, and now it seems unimaginable that school systems won't be altered radically as a result.

At Expo it became possible to envision a world in which all the resources previously available to private industries and show business – film, lighting, models, carefully organized environments – would be used by professional educators to bring new life to the school systems. And it became possible, also, to imagine a whole new future for the world's museums and art galleries, a future in which the art of display will become a profession in itself.

The people who made Expo set out to educate (or propagandize) their visitors in three separate ways: 1, Emotional displays, like the subliminal effects at Man In The Community; 2, Graphic effects, like the combination of films, moving models and flat illustrations at Man The Explorer; 3, Environmental effects, like the entrance to the British pavilion and the environments at the Western Provinces pavilion.

There was so much of this new, special education and propaganda going on, in fact, that a few old-fashioned displays, just by being blatantly traditional, turned out to be curiously memorable. The Cuban pavilion, a typographic nightmare of propaganda slogans (plus some very disorganized film) may have been objectionable, but its anti-American message was hardly forgettable. The Indians of Canada pavilion – where Canadian taxpayers paid, in effect, to be educated in how badly they had treated their native people – was equally effective. The signs on the walls were direct and unanswerable:

*An Indian child begins school by learning a foreign language. The White Man's school is an alien land for an Indian child.*

*The early missionaries thought we were pagans. They imposed on us their stories of God. But we spoke with God – the Great Spirit – in our own way.*

For the most part, however, education and propaganda at Expo were conveyed in fresh and imaginative styles. The "information cascade," as some display people like to call it, was prepared with enormous skill and ingenuity. But before any of this could happen, before the *how* of communication was determined, someone had to decide *what* Expo was to be all about.

The man who directed the most crucial development of Expo's message was Guy Dozois, the deputy director in charge of the theme pavilions. In a paper he wrote after all the work was done, Dozois described how Man – that is, an individual man, or woman – would or should feel when encountering Man And His World at Expo:

"Alone, he will learn to know himself better; he will scrutinize the world around him. Breathless, he will reflect upon the incredible advancements made within the last ten years. Spellbound, he will glimpse the future which awaits him. Infinitely small, he will stand at the centre of the universe, the microcosm within the macrocosm. But above all, he will sense that he, himself, is Man, the precious jewel around which everything turns."

That states the philosophy that might be called Expo-ism at its most delirious. The vanity of man has perhaps never been more specifically expressed than in those words, and this same vanity filled the very air one breathed at Expo. It is in the nature of world's fairs to be proud and optimistic, and Expo was no exception.

Richard D. Mandell, in his book *Paris 1900, The Great World's Fair*, surveyed the expositions of 19th-century France – in those days there was a major one about every eleven years – and concluded: "Most of all, the fairs themselves were manifestations of the positivists' faith in material and scientific progress as panaceas for all man's ills." Victor Hugo, in his salute to the 1867 Paris Exposition, insisted that it foretold a magnificent new Europe of peace and prosperity: "In the 20th century there will be an extraordinary nation . . . It will be illustrious, rich, thoughtful, peace-loving and friendly to the rest of humanity.

Vivid proof of progress in prosthetics – a man built of artificial limbs and organs.

A battle between Italians and Germans, between English and Russians, between Prussians and Frenchmen, will appear to it like a battle between the inhabitants of Picardy and Burgundy appears to us . . ."

This was 19th-century humanism as the great expositions expressed it. It was a failure, of course – the horrors of the 20th century sent it down in flames. But here we were at Montreal in 1967, celebrating it once more, in our century's most ingenious and most blatant expression of liberal optimism. You had the sense, wherever you turned, that the world's problems were being solved. Man The Provider was defeating starvation, and Man The Explorer was reaching to the ocean depths to provide riches for all of us. Man The Creator was expressing an elevated view of human existence, and Man The Producer was moving forward fearlessly on all fronts. The novelist Gabrielle Roy, who was considered the most eloquent voice at the 1963 thinkers' conference which established Expo's themes, was later to say of that meeting: "Firstly, one firm basis of accord was established: faith in progress." And Expo acted out this faith.

There were those who found the whole notion basically shallow. Barry Lord, an art critic and the editor of *arts/canada* magazine, wrote on the eve of the fair's opening: "If a world's fair had been held in Michelangelo's day, its theme might well have been Man And His World; that was the great age of humanism. But for a world's fair *today*, it would be difficult to conceive a less appropriate theme. For we live in a world in which humanist values are either wholly eclipsed, or rapidly vanishing . . . For further evidence that the concept behind Expo is awry, we might consider the fact that there is no pavilion of 'Man In War And Peace' included in the theme pavilions. Nor is there any reflection of the political alternatives of our time . . ."

But most of us wanted, with a sometimes touching desperation, to believe Expo's message, and sometimes our emotions helped us to do so. But even on the Expo site it was impossible to escape the fact that in some ways the world outside was steadily growing more miserable. One day the Swedish economist Gunnar Myrdal turned up at the Dupont Auditorium to give a lecture – an old-fashioned form of education that seemed strangely out of place – and told us that, for all this liberalism, the rich nations were now, by any reasonable measure, helping the poor nations *less* than they had a decade before. After that it was hard to return to Man the Liberal and take him seriously.

But it was even harder, perhaps, to suggest an alternative content for Expo's new forms of education. Liberalism of some kind remains, despite its monumental setbacks, the one philosophy modern man can go on with; Expo was right to adopt it, and to blind itself (most of the time) to the contradictions involved.

That this blindness was sometimes quite conscious emerged, two weeks before opening day, in the Incident of the Vanishing Picture. Man The Creator

Living lectures told part of the story of Man And The Oceans and Man The Producer.

had a huge collection of photographs from all over the world, and at least one of these, it developed, had political implications. To understand what happened, you have to know that a world's fair like Expo is a diplomatic event as well as an educational and commercial one. Invitations to take part are extended by the host government to national governments and all further relations – such as visits of heads of state – are arranged on the highest government level. At this level political feelings are sensitive, and the fact that Pierre Dupuy, the Commissioner-General, was a professional diplomat only added to the official air of the event. (Expo even had its own protocol department, so that when you were invited to an official party a young woman trilled, "Expo Protocol calling.")

The Incident of the Vanishing Picture began when one Ian Vorres, deputy commissioner-general of the Greek pavilion at Expo, picked up his copy of the Montreal *Star* for Monday, April 10. There he saw the anguished face of a Turkish Cypriot woman whose husband had just been killed by Greek soldiers. The caption explained this fact and noted that the picture was part of Expo's great photography show. Vorres was enraged.

"The photo itself," he said later, "was good as a photograph. But it was unfair and tactless to show it. It was a complete breach of the spirit of Expo to touch upon a thorny political issue."

Vorres protested to Expo. He threatened to keep his pavilion closed on the official opening day and he said the visit of the Greek royal family to Canada might be called off. Pierre Dupuy agreed with Vorres completely and decided the picture had to go. Furthermore, he specified that no pictures in the exhibition were to be identified in any way, except by title and name of photographer. The show's catalogue would eliminate all captions, so that nobody would be able to tell whether any other grieving women were Turks or Greeks or Norwegians or what. Dupuy officially apologized to Vorres, the honour of Greece was saved, and some of us received our most striking insight into the peculiar style of Expo.

In this one case, incidentally, suppression – as so often happens – had the opposite to the effect intended. By the time the controversy was over, the photograph had been reproduced in scores of Canadian newspapers, and always clearly identified. And when the Greek pavilion opened at least some of the visitors must have had in the backs of their minds the image of that stricken woman. Expo, it turned out, couldn't *quite* eliminate all unpleasantness. The real world of man occasionally broke in.

What was curious about the humanistic content of Expo was that it was alien to Roman Catholic culture. What had seemed from outside to be the most God-haunted, God-centred part of North America had now given birth to a national expression that was essentially man-centred. There was a Christian pavilion on the site, but its message (while handsomely conveyed) was so non-denominational that it came close to agnosticism. There was a Sermons From Science pavilion, preaching a fundamentalist religion, but it seemed altogether out of place. Expo made its message plain: Man is what is important in the world, Man is what makes things happen, Glory to Man in the Highest. In one theme section, devoted to Man In Control, a sign said: "The history of civilization is the story of man's struggle to control his world." It was a sign of Quebec's rapid change from priest-dominated to engineer-dominated society that everyone took that sort of message for granted. I saw exactly one letter in a French-Canadian newspaper objecting to Expo's humanism. The fair demonstrated something we had only guessed at before: Quebec was no longer, in the old sense, a Roman Catholic society. Like most of modern civilization, it had unconsciously changed religions.

The new religion – new to Quebec, at least – that was to govern Expo had been set forth in a paper prepared by the conference of Canadian intellectuals at Montebello. The paper outlined possible topics for theme pavilions and set forth a few general ideas about mankind: "The knowledge he has acquired of the world around him has brought modern man to a point where, having learned to escape the law of universal gravitation, the abilities he has developed now impel him to attack the evils which heretofore have been part and parcel of his existence; hunger and thirst, anxiety and war, suffering and disease, cold and drought, degrading labour, natural disaster, etc." Natural disaster, even! Victor Hugo could hardly have put it better.

The problem of bilingualism, so crucial to any modern Canadian institu-

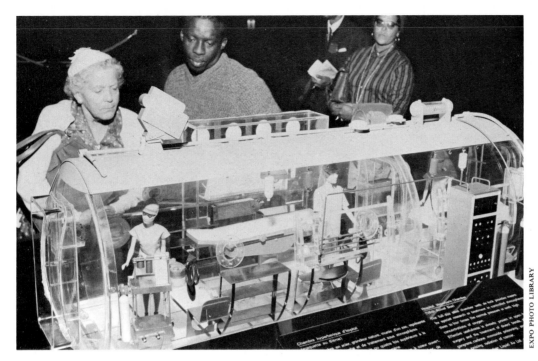

Expo tried to show it happening: the ideal operating theatre, sterile and partly automated.

tion, and so important in Montreal (which now has bilingual fortune cookies), may have partly inspired the educational *style* of Expo. For certainly it was, to an unprecedented extent, a *visual* exhibition. As the literary critic Hugh Kenner put it: "Expo 67, avoiding, where it can, words altogether, has funneled more energy into systematized non-verbal communication than any enterprise in the previous history of the world."

There were those, of course, who found Expo education a little hard to take. U.S. Senator Robert Kennedy, touring the site with wife and half a dozen children, declared at one point: "Enough of this educational stuff. Let's go to La Ronde and have some fun." (They liked the Flume Ride best.) Kenneth Tynan, the eminent British drama critic, declared that the Expo pavilions were "superb, ornate shells with rather hollow interiors." But for the crowds who lined up at Man In The Polar Regions, or the people who came two or three times to stand in line for Labyrinth, or the westerners who emerged with a deep sense of satisfaction from the Western Provinces pavilion, Expo education had meaning as well as style.

Some educational ideas that seem obvious in retrospect were actually revolutionary. Expo's hugely successful art gallery, in the Man The Creator section, was in effect a denial of all we have traditionally been taught about art history and art appreciation. The international committee that chose the works grouped them not according to periods or nations but according to themes – Man and Love, Man himself (meaning portraits), Man and His Conflicts, Man and Work – so that it became possible, for the first time in a show of masterpieces, to see how different cultures have treated the same subject. In the

154

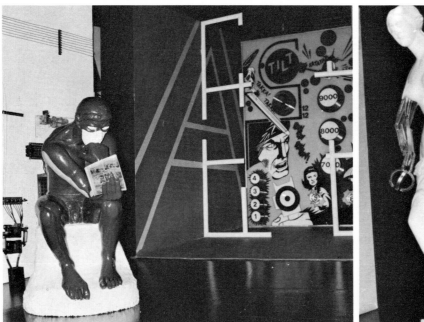

A pop-art Rodin's "Thinker" and a "Venus de Milo" with mechanical arms: two of the bizarre images in Man In The Community's Citérama exhibit symbolizing a city's varied life.

portraits section, an Egyptian granite statue of Amenhotep stood near a 13th-century Japanese courtier. In Man and Love, a 15th-century French tapestry showing courtly love was placed near a Van Dyck (family love) and a William Blake (spiritual love). It was all marvellously unexpected, and richly memorable. As the head of the Montreal Museum of Fine Arts put it, it was "an ultimate test of the conviction that fine things will always go together." The test was passed, and thousands of Expo visitors – many of them earlier brainwashed with the modern belief that in art, content hardly matters – experienced a fresh view of art and its meaning.

Man In The Community, the chief example of education-through-the-emotions, was intended also to provide a fresh view, this time of men living and working together. The point was not so much to introduce new information as to make us realize, consciously, what we already knew subconsciously.

Man In The Community was housed in a graceful wood-and-plastic pyramid designed by Arthur Erickson and Geoff Massey. In the centre of the pavilion was a pool of water, and directly above it (one hundred and forty feet up) the top of the pyramid was left open to the elements. Off this central core there were seven separate display rooms, and we moved from one to another. Citérama, the first, presented a rough, nerve-jangling Pop Art account of life in the modern city: You sat on little benches and these great unlikely images (Leonardo's ideal man, sketched in vulgar neon, the Venus de Milo with artificial arms attached, a sculpture covered in trading stamps), crashed past you as an insistent jazz score filled the air. Here was Man in Chaos. Then, moving deeper into the designers' environment, you walked into The Lonely Community, where a uniquely repellent display, inspired partly by the Toronto psychiatrist, Dr. Daniel Cappon, conveyed the idea of loneliness. Here were white plaster figures in cages, and as you looked at them stroboscopic lights blinked off and on, charging the environment with a nervous sense of urgency. As you stood there in the middle, something odd happened – you, your companions, and the others in the room seemed magically to change places with the lonely, isolated figures inside. The message was plain. (As the designer, Robin Bush, put it: "Who is in the cage? Visitor or visited?") Later, in the same pavilion, you were thrust into other environments: The Electronic Community, for instance, with its baffling images pushing themselves towards you, fighting for attention. It was all designed, as one of its organizers put it, as "a sort of immense 'Happening'," showing "how technological progress constrains Man to reconsider his environment."

By contrast, the kind of education represented by most exhibits in the two gigantic theme complexes – Man The Producer and Man The Explorer – tended to be specific rather than general, factual rather than emotional. But here, too, *involvement* was the key idea. You walked *into* the exhibits rather than just observing them. You played with a computer and got it to talk to you (though all it could really tell you was the date of your birth, after you had punched it out on a keyboard), you argued about English or French vocabulary with a teaching machine ("Try again!" it would say, very jolly and pleased with itself), you worked a TV camera that panned and zoomed all over the Expo grounds (for once, you could feel in control of the moving visual image before your eyes).

At Man And Life you walked into a human cell about one million times life size, looked through microscopes at single-celled animals multiplying before your eyes, watched a rat finding his way through a maze, and stared at an enormous model of the human brain lighting up in different sections as various emotions were signalled on the wall behind it. (Made of transparent plastic, twelve feet high and ten feet wide, that brain cost almost $200,000 and represented a dramatic forward step in the teaching of the human thought system.) At Man And His Health you could examine spare parts now being used for human beings, volunteer for a lie-detector test, and see filmed (and live-simulated) operations so graphic that some small fraction of every day's audience could be relied upon to faint, or vomit, or both. Involvement!

Sometimes these pavilions combined environmental design with specific factual information, and the result could be both stirring and informative. At Man And The Oceans you walked over an ocean bottom – actually, a glass floor, beneath which you could see coral, exotic plants, fish, old anchors – and at the same time heard the crash of surf and the cries of gulls. But then slowly you were introduced to factual information about how men explore the seas and use them. At one point you encountered a meteorological buoy, a device that records water temperatures and current velocities and radios them to a satellite above (if you looked up, incidentally, the satellite was there, too). To one side of the Oceans display were two diving vehicles, Saucer 300 and Saucer 4000, designed by Jacques-Yves Cousteau, with their "arms" and searchlights to be operated by aquanauts inside. In the middle of the exhibit was a diving tank where divers regularly demonstrated the history of their trade, from early sponge-gathering to Cousteau's live-at-the-bottom-of-the-sea experiments. From an underwater house a diver would emerge, gather fish, weld petroleum pipes, and pick up geological samples from the ocean floor. It all had about it the smell of reality, partly because it *was* to some extent "real" – the diver was actually there, doing all those things, even if it wasn't at the bottom of the ocean.

Where Man In The Community was emotional education and the other theme complexes were graphic-plus-environmental education, the Western Provinces pavilion put all its emphasis on environment. You started the pavilion with a thirty-second ride in a grim, rattling elevator designed to make you think you were going down into a mine. And at the end, there was the mine itself, smelling musty and nasty, badly lit. Later, towards the end of the pavilion, you emerged suddenly into the (real) outdoors and found yourself in a small corner of the British Columbia lumbering country, with a huge truck suddenly looming up beside you and a gigantic tree above you and mist coming from somewhere. A sense of *being there!*

But the underlying point of all the educational efforts at Expo was a sense of personal participation. This was post-textbook education: you didn't sit back and read something, you went there and walked through it, or played with it, or touched it, or anyway encountered it in some new way. This was what it was all about. Gabrielle Roy, in recalling those early discussions at Montebello, tried to set down one of the major points in the Canadian intellectuals' interpretation of Antoine de Saint-Exupéry's ideas:

"In the phrase Man's Earth we can appreciate the sense of order derived from each human being in his place – the teacher in her classroom, the shoemaker in his shop, the astronomer at Palomar. And who is to say which one is the most important in the final count of all the musicians who make up the orchestra? And how many in turn 'create' without knowing it! The child who invents his own game is creative; the mother who makes up a story for her sick child or a tasty dish for her harassed husband is creative. The nameless man coming home in the evening from office or factory amidst the teeming crowds is creative when he can still learn to believe in himself once more and in the Earth..."

The vision, of course, can be seen as hopelessly idealistic, pointlessly Utopian. Yet it has in it something of the genius of the human race, and it was this something that gave life and meaning to what we all experienced at Expo.

# The new look of learning

You walked through this model of a human cell magnified a million times, at the entrance to Man And Life Pavilion.

Education — from say-after-me-ABC to tours of musty museums which make the world seem dull – can never be the same. At Expo, you were not offered knowledge, but immersed in it.

# An enthralling lesson in how the brain controls us

The Man And Life Pavilion explained physiology with largely wordless demonstrations of how animal and human organs and faculties work. The third-floor brain, for instance: When a Laurel and Hardy sketch was projected on a screen, the fourteen-foot model laughed, and lit up like a computer's control panel.

The model brain symbolized the ultimate in human response: Reason. But it also laughed and cried and even grew angry.

# And a tour of the human body – with the aid of a rat in a maze

You were told nothing; shown everything: The start of life was a single-cell amoeba reproducing itself; instinct was a rat finding its way out of a maze; individuality was a group of monkeys responding differently to changing environments; the nerve-cell was a labyrinth of wiring. It all added up to a guided tour through the human body.

A web of cables, wires, plastic bulbs and flickering lights turned out to be a model of the neurons, the basic nerve cells which are the clearing house for the traffic of messages to and from the brain. It was part of a demonstration of how animals and humans receive information, then react either reflexively or – disciplined by the human brain – with intelligence.

As the adjoining screen glittered with pictures – perhaps of a man on a trapeze, or a golfer hitting a long one – the lights in the neuron model danced and the electrified mind came alive in its visual, audible demonstration of how the message relay centre functions. You were involved with the awesome, ineffably complex miracle of life.

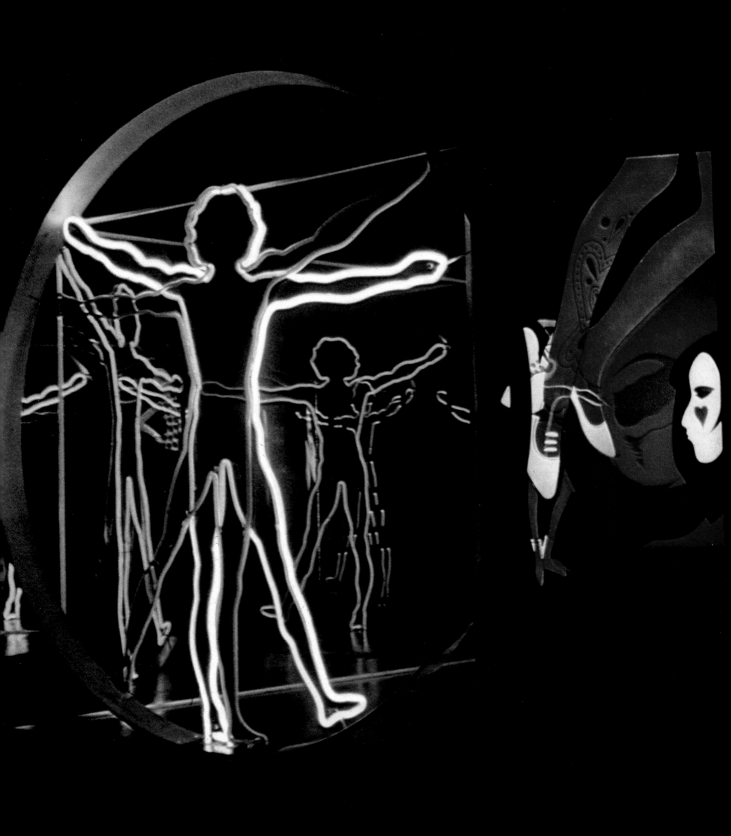

## Symbolism spells out the message

The displays at Man In The Community were a syllabus in symbolism, and the lesson was always stunningly, even brutally, clear: what was man doing with his inheritance? You stood, looked, listened, absorbed, and learned.

[*Left*] A silhouette of Da Vinci's perfect man. It was etched in neon to suggest perfection has become an artificial, empty shell.

[*Above, and right*] A tablet to trash — beer bottles, old phones, rusty autos make up a cynical bequest to posterity.

[*Right*] Man, lonely in a crowd, shut in a cage of his own making, unable to communicate with his fellows though the means — the symbolic telephone — are available. Artists who designed Man In The Community sought to involve visitors emotionally in humanity's problems. In what came to be called "the alienation room," stroboscopic lights flashed alternately on each exhibit, so its lesson was imprinted on the mind.

# Breaking the communications barrier

Displays like these in the Man And Life Pavilion which illustrated a child's burgeoning perceptive powers, will eventually be commonplace in schools, museums, even art galleries. Figures that move, trains that run, bring action and drama to the conveying of information. But, then, so did all the audio-visual, symbolic and subliminal teaching methods at Expo. They are more than gimmicks for getting attention: they may help man break through

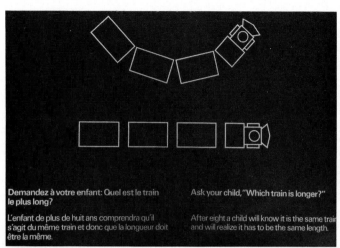

**Demandez à votre enfant: Quel est le train le plus long?**

L'enfant de plus de huit ans comprendra qu'il s'agit du même train et donc que la longueur doit être la même.

**Ask your child, "Which train is longer?"**

After eight a child will know it is the same train and will realize it has to be the same length.

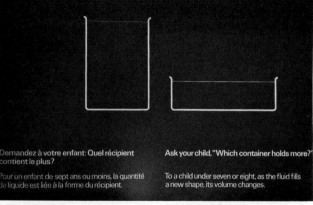

**Demandez à votre enfant: Quel récipient contient le plus?**

Pour un enfant de sept ans ou moins, la quantité de liquide est liée à la forme du récipient.

**Ask your child, "Which container holds more?"**

To a child under seven or eight, as the fluid fills a new shape, its volume changes.

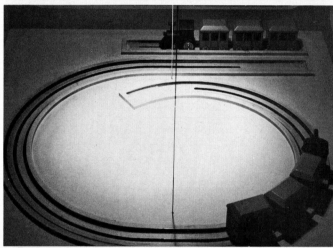

This mechanical doll answered its own question by pouring the same quantity of water into each container in a visible lesson for the young.

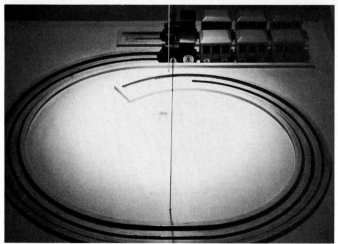

The trains responded to their own question. The one on the circular track moved so that every few minutes they met and demonstrated the answer.

the comprehension barrier thrown up by the knowledge explosion. In our world, we know more and more about less and less: a physicist can only be understood by another physicist; even TV repairmen and professional

footballers have a special language. The new teaching techniques at Expo sparked imaginations. Their aim was to help child and man understand – and make them *want* to understand – ideas otherwise beyond their comprehension.

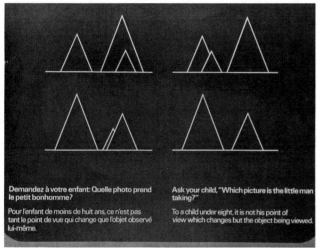

Demandez à votre enfant: Quelle photo prend le petit bonhomme?

Pour l'enfant de moins de huit ans, ce n'est pas tant le point de vue qui change que l'objet observé lui-même.

Ask your child, "Which picture is the little man taking?"

To a child under eight, it is not his point of view which changes but the object being viewed.

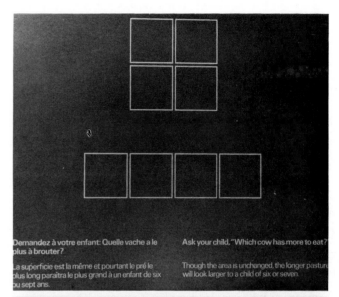

Demandez à votre enfant: Quelle vache a le plus à brouter?

La superficie est la même et pourtant le pré le plus long paraîtra le plus grand à un enfant de six ou sept ans.

Ask your child, "Which cow has more to eat?"

Though the area is unchanged, the longer pasture will look larger to a child of six or seven.

This was one of the few static perception tests, but it, too, was a visual problem, not just a stated (and therefore abstract) question.

Pour les jeunes enfants, tout changement dans la forme ou la place d'un objet est susceptible d'en modifier la nature même: l'objet devient un autre objet.

To young children the identity of an object is not preserved as it changes shape and position, it becomes a different object.

The tiny figure moved around the display case, changing the question. The very presence of movement guaranteed a child's attention.

ACTUALLY BEING THERE ... In the Western Provinces Pavilion you went past a routine tableau of prairie life into a simulated rain forest, complete with a brutally big, and real, logging truck. Nothing could have made you realize more clearly the size and importance of Canada's timber industry.

# 9 | Self portraits: true and false

A world's fair in the 1960s is a place to display images rather than facts. No one building can tell you all about a society, but it can tell you how a people – or their leaders – want their society to appear. At Expo the Americans chose to present themselves as youthful, innocent, playful. The Russians wanted to impress us with the sheer weight of their technology; their display resembled a gigantic hardware store. The Czechs who run a pretty closed society at home, seemed to want us to believe their country was rich, open, even *gay*.

The whole issue of images came spectacularly into the open in two quite memorable contrasts: Ontario versus Quebec, and Britain versus France. The fact that these pavilions were all in one place, ranged in a row along the edge of Ile Notre Dame, made the contrasts all the more effective.

There they stood, side by side, the pavilions of the two richest Canadian provinces, separated by only a few yards of water. Individually they were interesting, but together they made a fascinating study: Ontario robust and creative and perhaps a little awkward; Quebec, by contrast, cool and restrained and sophisticated. A Quebec journalist said to me: "The Ontario pavilion is like the Quebec people, and the Quebec pavilion is like the Ontario people." It was as if the two provinces had for some reason decided to exchange identities.

After a moment, of course, the reason came clear. Ontario wanted to destroy its traditional image – tough, efficient, money-grabbing, the industrial centre of Canada; it wanted to look freer, more open. Quebec, by contrast, wanted to abolish its rural, religion-dominated, old-world image; it wanted to suggest that it, too, had entered the modern world and knew what technology was all about.

In 1964, when it finally became clear to everyone that there was actually to *be* an Expo, Ontario threw itself into the project enthusiastically. It acquired the fifth largest site at Expo and planned the sixth largest pavilion (in the end it was to cost $8.5 millions). To prepare a theme, the government's special pro-

The brooding revolutionary Vladimir Lenin set the atmosphere in Russia's Pavilion.

jects branch hired a sophisticated team of experts in communications, among them the journalist Barbara Moon and the television producer Ross McLean. As architects it commissioned the firm of Fairfield and DuBois, which had been responsible, among other things, for the famous theatre at Stratford, Ontario. Macy DuBois, who designed the pavilion, said later that he received his original inspiration when he was standing in the middle of an open space at the Joie de Vivre Pavilion at the 1964 fair in Lausanne, Switzerland.

"The noon bells of a little church in the pavilion were ringing," he recalled, "and there were a great many people listening to them this day. But there was no sense of a crowd. It was just a lot of people moving freely through a beautifully sculptured space, experiencing a marvellous moment. The pavilion itself was quite simple, but it made the best use of space I've seen in a 20th-century building. And that's the idea that stuck in my mind because I knew then that there was one really crushing problem facing everyone at Expo: not enough room. Just too much, too closely together."

At that point DuBois knew the problem that faced him and, for that matter, most of the architects at Expo. (Of course no one knew, till the fair opened, just how much overcrowding Expo's success would create.) DuBois decided to solve it with a pavilion open on all sides, where visitors could have a free, unprogrammed experience. Freedom: that became the central idea, and the result was one of the most pleasant, most relaxed of all the Expo buildings. The people

The United States settled for Humphrey Bogart's weary worldliness.

didn't march through it in orderly ranks – as in, say, the Czech pavilion. Rather, they strolled, taking it easy.

DuBois created a pedestrian walk in the middle of his pavilion and, eighteen feet above it, an exhibit floor. He put in ramps rather than stairs, to lead visitors gently, casually upward. He made his structure a complex assembly of steel girders covered with a vinyl-coated fibreglass. It looked, as a newspaperman wrote, like "a bat struggling under a sheet"; certainly there was nothing graceful about it, but you had to admit it had identity – it didn't look like anything else at Expo, or, for that matter, like anything else in the world.

The sense of a relaxed environment was even more evident in the handling of the great granite cubes – in all, 10,292 tons of stone – piled around the pavilion in irregular patterns, and in the gleaming mirror-like Walking Women sculptures by Michael Snow, dotted through the pedestrian areas. People sat on the granite cubes to eat picnic lunches, and children climbed over them. As the minirail soared overhead – and, at one point, went right through the pavilion – it was obvious DuBois had succeeded.

There were surprises all over the Ontario grounds. Ontario traditionally has maintained repressive drinking laws, yet the Ontario bar was as comfortable as any at Expo – indeed, I thought it the *most* comfortable. Ontario doesn't allow its citizens to drink outdoors – there is believed to be something shameful about people actually drinking in full view of the public, where even children might see them – yet the Ontario pavilion had an outdoor restaurant where people sat eating and drinking, apparently without harm to anyone. A side effect of Expo was that the Ontario Government, apparently embarrassed by the fact that its pavilion restaurants and bars would have to be open on Sunday, for the first time loosened its own laws to make public drinking on Sunday permissible, though only with meals. In this case, image-building worked backwards, the Expo image affecting the reality back home.

In the exhibit spaces, the Ontario image was – as one of the hackneyed words of the 1960s has it – *swinging*. The Teen Scene section was all blinking tail-lights and electric guitars and rock music; a television set ran endlessly, showing teenagers at their tribal dances. Children were represented by a handsome children's art exhibit in which Batman and snowmen hung side by side. The Gross Provincial Product was portrayed in Op Art columns. Electric power was represented by a "camp" item, a 1912 truck of the kind used to sell Ontario on public power, and – if that jargon can be qualified – an even more camp display showed 19th-century Ontario through ancient streetlights, old livestock posters, and a penny farthing bicycle. A collection of bilingual talking robots represented the working world: characters like Miss Arts and Letters (whose torso was a cello) and Mr. Business (telephone dials for eyes, a stapler for a nose) discussed careers. The other exhibits celebrated old-fashioned rocking horses and a discount-house merchant, art collecting and nuclear power. And, of course, there was Christopher Chapman's multi-image film, *A Place to Stand*, which many of us regarded as one of the most memorable achievements at Expo.

The total impression was uneven, a little junky, certainly bizarre.

Next door, at the Quebec pavilion, everything was radically different. The building, first, was a superb example of cool modern architecture. The architects – Papineau, Gerin-Lajoie and LeBlanc, with Luc Durand as associate – created a huge glass house, surrounded on all sides by water and reached by a footbridge. In the daytime the blue-tinted walls reflected the fair around – the Ontario pavilion on one side, the French on the other, the minirail as it went by. At night they became transparent and through them you saw the blinking lights inside.

Like Macy DuBois of Ontario, the Quebec architects brought something important back from Lausanne's 1964 fair. What they acquired there was not an idea but a person: Gustave Maeder, a 39-year-old Swiss designer. At Lausanne, Maeder worked on graphic design for the transportation and communication section and the aviation exhibit. At Expo his spirit took over the Quebec pavilion and made it a kind of art object.

Two decades ago, as a young painter, Maeder idolized Piet Mondrian, the most severe of all the important modern artists. Today Mondrian's hard-edge style continues to dominate Maeder's visual imagination, and it dominated all

With all those hostesses, a contest was inevitable. Miss Britain [fourth from left, seated] won.

the work he did at Montreal. Maeder – whose contribution, incidentally, was entirely ignored by the press in Quebec – filled the pavilion with 4,200 two-foot wooden cubes, painted in pure colours. The cubes were piled up into pillars, stuck together to make walls, used as display cases for films and still photos. The result was intensely stylish and sophisticated, the most rarefied design image at Expo.

Maeder's work suited what the Quebec Provincial Government wanted to put in its pavilion; as a government press release put it, his style emphasized "sobriety and efficiency." There were to be few references to religion, very little folklore, very little history. Fine art was pushed into a corner on the top floor. Instead, the pavilion concentrated on industry and city life, on technology and higher education. There were references to lumbering (one pile of Maeder cubes was frozen in the act of falling, like a chopped-down tree) and there was a brief, remarkable film on water power. But these traditional parts of the Quebec image were treated in the most sophisticated way possible. Otherwise, there was an emphasis on *modern* forms of money-making that would have shocked an earlier generation of Quebeckers. The purpose, as the same press release said, was "to illustrate the many aspects of human activity which have enabled the Quebec people to raise themselves to the rank of an industrial nation."

You entered the pavilion proper by a slowly moving circular elevator. "A moment of darkness," the hostess at the controls said, and everything was black. Then you were suddenly in an abstract evocation of the Quebec wilderness: mirrors multiplied to infinity a series of stylized tree-shapes, and the effect was spectacular. Then, when you left the elevator, you were among Maeder's cubes and their elaborate contents – fifteen different films, luminous panels, photographs, reproductions of a few ancient documents. There was no humour, there was no surprise – just a steadily increasing sense of achievement and pride. And behind it all, or accompanying it, was an electronic sound track put together by the leading French-Canadian composer Gilles Tremblay. A mixture of bird songs and grinding machines, of mine explosions and howling storms, of pure electronic sounds and bubbling brooks, it charged the building with an insistent modernity.

If Ontario and Quebec represented the eccentric image versus the sophisticated, then Britain and France, just down the street, represented satire versus solemnity.

In the confusion of Expo, the weird collection of shapes and colours and ideas and facts, it was possible after a while to pick out a certain dominating spirit. It was there somehow in the minirail, and in the triangular wastebaskets, and in the gondolas gliding through the lagoons. It was in the C.P.R.-Cominco film, *We Are Young*, and in the film *Urbanissimo* at Man In The Community. The United States pavilion had it, and so did Ontario's. You could see it in parts of the Italian pavilion, and certainly in the Czech. Quebec just missed it (not by much) and the Soviet Union missed it entirely. Cuba, for all its propaganda bombast, managed to achieve it. Britain achieved it most of all.

It was, above all, a light-hearted spirit, a determination not to take issues and facts too seriously, not to press too heavily on the visitor's tolerance of pomposity. At the British pavilion the spirit began with the Pop Art version of the Union Jack stuck on top of the two-hundred-foot tower of Sir Basil Spence's otherwise ponderous, castle-like pavilion, whose walls, while made of a kind of cardboard, looked like stone. (Roy Strong, director of Britain's National Portrait Gallery, wrote in the London *Spectator* that Sir Basil's building seemed "very Thirties, closely allied to the architecture at the opening of Movietone News, only minus the searchlight beams piercing the night sky. One expected Noel and Gertie to saunter out dreamy in chiffon.")

The spirit was dominant inside, in the most talked-about of the exhibits. As Expo opened, the correspondent of the Doncaster *Evening Post* reported: "The stuffy image Britain once presented to the world is to be swept away for good at Expo 67." And so it proved to be, for those five million people who endured the line-ups and made their way through the British pavilion. The line-ups here, incidentally, were exceptionally long, because: 1, The pavilion was so popular; 2, The people moved through it so slowly. On rainy days the

## Who's Who at the big fair

The glamorous, rich and powerful came to Expo. Among them: General de Gaulle, Princess Margaret and her husband, President Lyndon Johnson [who seems less than enraptured with Commissioner General Pierre Dupuy], Prince Rainier and Princess Grace, the **Shah of Iran** and a hip Jacqueline Kennedy.

hostesses issued black umbrellas to the first few hundred people in line.

Inside there were, of course, some of the usual solemn exhibits: Industrial Britain, all about automation and other new techniques the British aren't supposed to be good at; Britain in the World, a section dominated by enormous and hideous sculptured figures, under which you could listen through telephones to boring descriptions of how the British had invented or propagated almost everything of any value; and The Genius of Britain, an endless collection of still pictures of everybody from Isaac Newton to Emmeline Pankhurst. But somehow no one ever noticed these things, or anyway no one talked about them afterwards. What we all remember instead were the introduction to the pavilion and the section called Britain Today, each of them in its own way unforgettable.

The introduction, titled Shaping the Nation, was brilliantly conceived by the stage designer Sean Kenny (whose $3 million fun-ride at La Ronde, the Gyroton, was a sad flop). You walked in out of the sunlight and suddenly you were standing on a moving platform going through a kind of cave. All around you there was water, and simulated rocks, and on the rocks were projected images – kings, bishops, knights, peasants, Vikings, Roman legionnaires. There was burning and rioting and killing; on the sound track you could hear chanting and shouting and screaming and the clash of sword against sword. It was a new kind of mass communication, a sort of animated environment, and some of us found it the most beautifully programmed six minutes at Expo. At the end, of course, you didn't know what king had killed his brother or which bishops had Christianized whom; you had, rather, a sort of *idea* of how it all went, because in a sense you had been there.

But what followed upstairs, in Britain Today, was even more remarkable. James Gardner, who designed it, had designed solemn exhibitions in the past (Britain's at Brussels in 1958, for instance) but this time he had the revolutionary notion of transferring to a national pavilion the kind of humour that is commonplace on television and in magazines and stage revues.

First, he laid it out like a film studio, with all lights unconcealed, with no crowd-movements charted. You just sort of wandered around, taking in one piece of information (or humour) at a time. Gardner did away with formal design entirely. "I've thrown away design and concentrated on content," he explained. "The design takes care of itself."

The content was as varied as Britain itself. There was a hedgerow right out of a 19th-century British print, but there was also a section devoted to the Beatles. There was a cinematic view of the English countryside (you saw it by looking down a well), but there was also a collection of Pop and Op art by British artists still unknown (some of them deservedly so). There was a sculptured English family, very traditional, but with a television crew whose camera was trained on them – the TV people representing mass communications.

Gardner's exhibit had a peculiar effect on visitors: they wanted to *show* it to each other. You could stand there and watch each person discover it for himself, then go off to another side of the room and drag his companion over to point out this or that detail. In one place a cutaway model of an apartment house showed every family watching the same football game on TV, illustrating the point that soccer in Britain appeals to all classes and ages. In two other places little old ladies sat knitting while watching on TV a brief, constantly repeated film of the Duke of Edinburgh – sailing, playing polo, and smiling, smiling, smiling. (In each case actual film was shown on the TV sets, and the response to it indicated one aspect of the Expo revolution. A decade ago such use of film would have been sensationally effective, but at Expo it was simply accepted as part of the overall design.)

In one corner a collection of sculptured figures depicting pompous young university people were shown talking earnestly about their future in the new scientific Britain ("Let's leave C.P. Snow out of this," one of them said.) A car, decorated in Union Jack style, was accompanied by a sign, *We love our car*, and a teapot by a sign, *We like our cup of tea*.

The result, Gardner admitted, "is unorthodox and may even be misunderstood, but its existence amid the pomp and circumstance of a world fair will at least demonstrate the British virtue of tolerance, of live and let live."

Against that remark, set this quotation from a press release covering part of the French pavilion's section on raw materials and energy: *The Le Havre methane port consists of three reservoirs of 423,600 cu. ft. each, with an inner tank made of steel alloy (9% nickel) 82 sq. ft. in diameter and 98 ft high.*

Now that's the way it was at the French pavilion: all facts, *big* facts. Where the British set out to charm you, the French overwhelmed you with detail. (There were, as it turned out, few line-ups at the French pavilion.) The building itself, designed by Jean Faugeron and Andre de Mot, in what the pavilion officials were pleased to call "lyric architecture," was spiky and ungainly but nevertheless emphatic. It had the look of an architectural student's just-fooling-around model that had been suddenly and unexpectedly blown up to full scale. And as it happened, models *were* the main contents of the French pavilion.

Outside there was a scale model of the French Diamant rocket, designed to launch satellites, and inside there was a scale model of just about everything else that France produces, expects to produce, or just wishes it could produce – the Concorde supersonic aircraft, the S.S. *France*, the tanker *Jules Verne* ("since 1965, this vessel has carried the equivalent of over 1.5 billion cubic feet of liquid natural gas each month from Arzew to Le Havre"), the Alouette 3 helicopter, three French nuclear power stations, a new telephone switching machine, an infra-red laser transmitter, a bathyscape, the hydropneumatic suspension system of the Citroen, *everything*. One had the sense that every model-maker in France had been working on this project for years.

And everywhere there was an expression of pride: in French streets, French railroads, French art, French countryside. Visitors to the pavilion were heard sometimes expressing wonderment at the notion that France would actually *boast* about any aspects of the notorious French telephone system, but in fact there it was – an entire exhibit telling how great it's going to be, one day, to make a phone call in France.

The tone throughout was solemn, satisfied, humourless. If Britain needed charm to win its way in the world, this contrast suggested, France emphatically did not; it had power instead.

In the great well of the building – the floors full of exhibits were arranged around an open space – there was a work of what artists sometimes call "mixed media." Here a six-minute electronic music performance was synchronized with flashing lights and abstract colour slides; the effect was both startling and intimidating.

Only on the terrace, above the vast collection of models and graphs and maps and charts, was there a touch of humour; and the humour was remarkably neurotic. The sculptors Jean Tinguely and Niki de Saint-Phalle had collaborated on a "fantastic garden," 2,000 square feet, in which sculptures representing the Masculine Principle (Tinguely's) and the Feminine Principle (Saint-Phalle's) fought out the war of the sexes, all day long. Tinguely's sharp-edged kinetic metal objects attacked, probed, pushed, *raped* the bulbous pastel-coloured plaster figures of Saint-Phalle, whose only defence was to be as ugly as possible.

"We collaborated, each one against the other," Tinguely told me when I encountered him among his sculptures on opening day. He and *Mlle* Saint-Phalle had collaborated before, but he imagined they wouldn't be working together again; apparently they began to take their sculptures' combat seriously. The result of their work was perhaps the world's most outlandish sculpture show; the truly remarkable aspect of it was that someone – *two* people, in fact – had gone to the trouble of making these appalling objects.

France's image at Expo doesn't, of course, tell us everything about the people of the place where the image was created; nor does Britain's or Ontario's or Quebec's. Just as a politician's image may be only what his speechwriters want us to see, so a country's image at a world fair may represent no more than a notion cherished by a few well-placed bureaucrats, a few talented (or untalented) architects and designers. But by the time Expo had closed its turnstiles many of us, Canadians and foreigners, had been afforded some revelatory glimpses into the psychology of our fellow citizens of this earth.

# The image makers

The faces they showed the world: Quebec Pavilion [*left*] looked severe, efficient; Ontario's [*right*] seemed gay, romantic.

Expo was not, perhaps, always an accurate reflection of Man and His World. Bent on image building, the peoples presented themselves as they'd *like* others to see them. Russia isn't as joylessly technological, nor Jamaica so frivolous, nor India so earnest, as their pavilions suggested. There were also undertones of national policies: the French Pavilion reflected the haughty grandeur of the Gaullist dream; the British insisted they were abandoning their love affair with yesterday. For Canadians, the puzzle between the Expo image and everyday reality was best posed at the Quebec and Ontario pavilions. Quebec's was functional, even dour; Ontario's was sophisticated, even uninhibited. In the *argot* of the moment, French Canada came through as "square," while English Canada seemed to emerge as really "swinging."

## Ontario

Blocks of rock tumbled beneath the pavilion proper, symbolizing the wilderness of the Canadian Shield. Truly symbolic – but relaxing enough to be popular with skylarking children and picnicking families.

## Quebec

Cubic inside and out, it provided the sought-after image of "sobriety and efficiency." Its walls of cube-like glass were tinted. By day, they were mirrors; by night, inside lights transformed them into windows.

## Ontario

For its Teen Scene display, Ontario designers piled up a chaotic collage – a gleaming mess of auto parts, sports gear, musical instruments that were all once used by teenagers. The pavilion had zip and style.

## Quebec

This symbolic pine forest was designed to demonstrate the rugged terrain and harsh climate over which the French Canadians have triumphed in much of *la Belle Province.* It worked, but you couldn't call it groovy.

## How the French see themselves: cool and elegant

The theme was Gallic tradition and invention: floor after floor of the sciences, planning, art and literature. It was a multi-tiered display of prestigious achievement . . . but where was the haunting romance of the Ile de France?

The Polytope filled the pavilion's core with a web of cables bearing 1,200 bulbs. To a computer's rigid commands, electronic music played, lights danced, while fountains of lacy water rose and fell with exact obedience.

The French rocket pointed a proud, powerful finger skyward.

Sensual statuary graced the fifth "level of achievement."

# How the British see themselves: mod and merry

We believe in laughing at ourselves

However professional we become, we respect the inspired amateur
........................................
Quel que soit notre talent nous respectons l'amateur éclairé

We believe in the Englishness of roses

We believe in puddings

For every baby there are five budgies
........................................
Cinq fois plus de perruches que de bébés

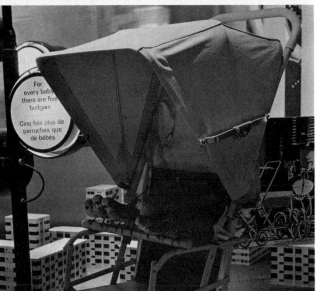

Central heating of a kind widely in use throughout Britain. Puddings keep the cold out, too.

However humble, his home is still his castle, but an Englishman's heart is often in his garden.

With irreverent items, the British poked wry fun at themselves. So old-line immigrants didn't always get the

The British Lion pulled its own tail with a pavilion that refused to take itself or its people too seriously. The 200-ft. tower, with a three-dimension Union Jack on the top, dominated Ile Notre Dame, and the displays skipped over a history of conquest and discovery which shaped much of the world to concentrate on "The Challenge of Change" – how a Britain, no longer quite as Great, struggles, often in some pain, to catch up with the 20th century.

Upper crust meets miniskirt – a search for the compromise that will keep the best of the old to strengthen the new.

Really, a mile of steam vapour? On the jigsaw wall [*right*], Union Jack seems scissored — and can that be a Yankee star?

**Philosophy in art:
the presence
of a greater being?**

The giant aluminum figures by
Mario Armengol dominated
the fifth and last chamber of
the British Pavilion. These
weird, compelling beings
inspired conflicting moods
in visitors: first, of man
dominating the world, and then
of man himself dwarfed.

# 10 | Just fifteen millions extra

*Because a train will transport* (the Expo visitor) *around the grounds without charge, his feet will pain him less than at any other major fair in recent history. Nor will he have to waste hours in queues; computers will digest information about lines and flash the minute-by-minute situation onto big electronic tote boards. ("Skip the British Pavilion. Crowded," the boards might read.)*

– Life, *April 28, 1967.*

*Throughout the exhibition site, electronic tote boards announce which pavilions have waiting lines, while reservation booths dispense advance tickets to the more popular free shows. At the first sign of a queue, closed-circuit TV cameras flash an alarm to an underground control center, which dispatches a jeep bearing troubadours, jugglers and other time-passers to the critical area.*

– Newsweek, *May 1, 1967.*

O trusting *Life*! O naive *Newsweek*! O optimistic Expo! In those last heady days before the fair opened, when the articles quoted above were written, the miracle of Expo's construction had come to pass and now anything, anything! was possible. Having failed to believe in the original idea of Expo, various journalists, like converts to a church, now decided to accept every word of the Expo dogma, however outlandish. But much of it was – accidentally – lies, lies…

Things just didn't work out that way. The problem of crowd control totally defeated the best efforts of the Expo staff. People who had built a magnificent fair in an unthinkably short time were first embarrassed and then baffled by the problem of how to move hundreds of thousands of people from here to there. By the time Expo was a month old it was evident to everyone that this was Expo's greatest failure.

The failure was born, of course, out of Expo's success. Expo expected 35 million people; 50 millions came. On the first weekend there wasn't enough food, or transport, or space; there weren't enough groundskeepers to keep the place clean. Some of these problems could be solved by the Expo staff:

Expo bars and restaurants were too small, too crowded, too few, and [usually] too expensive.

they could hire more groundskeepers, for instance. Some could be solved by the visitors themselves: they could bring picnic lunches and thereby avoid the over-crowded and (often) over-priced restaurants. But in the end nobody could do anything about line-ups.

Reservexpo, to which that innocent *Newsweek* writer referred, was to be a system by which visitors could avoid line-ups at the most favoured shows, like Labyrinth and the Telephone pavilion. You would arrive early at Expo, go to one of the information kiosks, and ask for free reserved tickets to the shows you wanted to see. A computer would tell the hostess behind the desk whether tickets were available, and she would issue them to you. Simple as that.

But the system quickly fell apart. Each conversation between visitor and hostess seemed to take forever, and long queues began forming at each kiosk. Visitors found themselves lining up, for as much as two hours, in order to avoid *other* line-ups; and, while standing waiting, they had no idea whether any tickets for what they wanted to see would be awaiting them at the head of the line. One woman lined up for two hours only to be told there were no more reservations for anything; she slapped the hostess in the face. Esso, which sponsored the kiosks, began to see that in public relations terms they were, as the military men say, counter-productive. On June 21 the system, only a few weeks old, closed down completely.

That electronic bulletin board which *Life* celebrated in advance was another failure. In this case, visitors simply proved resistant to suggestions – if the board said the British pavilion was crowded, people went there anyway, knowing it was worth seeing. Labyrinth had line-ups four hours long while the nearby Man In The Community was sometimes nearly empty – because the people wanted to see Labyrinth, and didn't care if they never saw Man In The Community.

With tables booked up for weeks, most visitors soon gave up on the gourmet attractions.

As for those travelling "troubadours, jugglers and other time-passers" – well, they, too, proved counter-productive. When an entertainer came along to amuse people in a line-up he merely drew *more* people.

At Expo there were several agents of Osaka's Expo '70 who wanted to know what their fair's greatest problem would be. By the time they went home to go to work, they knew the answer: crowd control.

If nearly everything that went wrong on the Expo site was the result of success, almost everything that went wrong off the site was the result of incompetence. Long before Expo opened, critics opposed to the whole idea insisted that Montreal wouldn't be able to sleep, comfortably, the millions of people who would be coming to see the fair. This turned out to be true, but not for the reasons everyone anticipated. What went wrong was the elaborate system of planning, called Logexpo, by which the fair's organizers had hoped to arrange for the accommodation of out-of-town visitors.

The idea was to organize every kind of reservation – in hotels, motels, boarding houses, private homes – under a single system, computerize it, and thus use completely every available room. But somehow it didn't work. The computers ("penetration analysis system," the bureaucrats called them) just didn't work, or maybe the human beings running them didn't know what to do with them. In any case it became obvious, even before the opening on April 28, that something was going wrong. On April 16, the New York *Times* printed a letter from a man in Hartford, N.Y.

"If you do another piece on Expo 67, you should know that today I sent off my fourth request to Logexpo for accommodations in May. I started in January. Over half the time to my visit has elapsed, yet to date I have received either no answer or nothing more than published literature in reply. Each time

I asked for specific lodging, dates, rates . . . I was quite prepared to send a deposit cheque if I only knew where to send it. Now I have decided not to go, and am advising employees of my company to do likewise."

That was only the beginning. After Expo opened, the complaints grew more numerous and more bitter. When Logexpo finally got around to answering its mail, the answers were frequently more harmful than helpful. It became obvious that Logexpo had set its standards much too low, and was involved in perpetrating a kind of fraud. Would-be visitors to Expo would receive brochures showing handsome motel rooms available for $22 a night per couple. They would send off their deposits – often $50 or more – and then arrive in Montreal expecting something like a Holiday Inn. Instead they would find themselves lodged in temporary motels that resembled, in design and facilities, rather primitive army barracks. Naturally, they would ask for their money back. Naturally, the motel owners would refuse to hand it over.

In the first weeks of the fair the Montreal Better Business Bureau was receiving fifty complaints a day from people in this situation. As spring and summer wore on the correspondence columns of the Montreal newspapers filled up with complaints from out-of-town visitors who had gone home enraged. On July 10 the Montreal *Star* carried a letter from a man in Fairfax, Virginia:

"Responding to the high-promise advertisements, my wife and I sent an application and specifications before the exposition opened, and were assigned a motel to which we sent a prompt deposit. Some time later we were informed by the motel management that due to overbooking it was necessary to transfer us to a new apartment, where we would share a bath. We wrote immediately – copy to Logexpo – cancelling the reservation and asking for our money back. Four months and a number of letters have passed and at last we have been promised that our money will be returned. Just a promise, no money yet.

"When the first motel let us down we immediately asked Logexpo to get us another, since we had been led to believe it had been set up to protect the public from shady deals. After long delay and correspondence we were assigned to another motel and made a deposit there.

"We arrived in Montreal and found our second motel to be a green-lumber structure emerging from a stumpy swamp. There were no covers on the bed, no towels and no place to hang a shred of clothing. The shower stall was a rattling metal affair with exposed pipes. The manager screwed hooks into the walls as maids made the beds and we unpacked. The advertised television set – a second-hand one – came after we had gone to bed that night.

"Outside, a thin cover of crushed stone had been spread over the soft muck, and wheels were beginning to sink as rains came. For this we paid $22 per night and we were afraid not to; we had to have a place to stay . . ."

Failure to provide for queues was an Expo blooper. This Labyrinth line-up was four hours long.

That letter was so typical the *Star* headed it: "One More Complaint For The Dossier." But the low point was still to come: On August 8 the United States Post Office announced it had instructed employees to reject all mail addressed to something called the Canadiana 67 Motel on Dorchester Boulevard East, in Montreal. That, it turned out, was a motel approved by Logexpo.

A Washington journalist, Stanley Cohen, had stayed at the Canadiana 67 a few weeks earlier. Like other visitors he had been led to expect normal modern motel standards. He found instead that his room ($26 for two adults and a child) had no telephone and no cross ventilation; from the outside the building looked like a customs shed in an under-developed country. Cohen's documented complaint, added to others, had forced the Post Office to act. It ordered all mail addressed to Canadiana 67 to be returned to the sender, stamped FRAUDULENT.

By then Logexpo's reputation had reached bottom. At the beginning of the fair, twenty-five per cent of tourists seeking accommodation in Montreal used Logexpo; by early August the figure was down to seven per cent. There were successful prosecutions for fraud, producing small fines for motel owners. Nothing anybody could do could rescue the situation. Logexpo wasn't a failure; it was a disaster.

Expo, in its successes and failures, demonstrated that the historic timing of a world's fair is crucial to the quality of its contents. Expo happened to arrive at a moment when architecture, for instance, was alive with new and challenging ideas, and some of these the fair accurately reflected. It came at a time when the movies were on the edge of new discoveries – and these, too, Expo demonstrated. But, judging by the evidence on the site, this moment in history did not find sculpture in a particularly happy situation. Or, in any case, not the kind of sculpture Expo wanted – that is, monumental sculpture.

Where Expo exhibited the sculpture of the past, even the recent past – as in its great art exhibit, or the outdoor sculpture show near the U.S. pavilion – its purpose was fulfilled: here were the riches of the world, spread out before the visitors, as they should have been. Where Expo, on the other hand, showed the sculpture of the present, or where it showed sculpture made for this occasion, there was a sense of disappointment and emptiness. Many of the national pavilions showed recent sculpture – Italy, Germany, France, the Scandinavian countries – and in most cases it was mediocre. The two countries now most important in world sculpture, the United States and Britain, showed only one piece each. The Swiss, as if resigned to this situation, consigned the great master Alberto Giacometti to a meagre five-piece exhibition, badly arranged, behind their pavilion.

If the foreign sculptors were in general mediocre, the Canadians were

When it rained, thousands got wet. More shelter against storms should have been provided.

frequently very bad. So what should have been, by all the rules, the easiest art for Expo to handle – since each piece is self-contained, and since each creator works on his own – turned out to be the fair's most spectacular artistic failure.

*Man*, Alexander Calder's largest work ever, was commissioned by Expo, paid for by International Nickel, and planned as not only one of the great artistic events of the fair but also as a kind of symbol of its purpose. *Man* stands sixty-seven feet high on Ile Ste. Hélène (it has been donated to the city, and will stay on the site permanently), and from most angles it looks simply terrible: a great knobby chunk of steel, an ungracious mass of ungainly angles, a totally earthbound work of art. Calder is an American sculptor of considerable distinction, but what Expo and Inco forgot was that (1) his reputation is for mobiles, not stabiles; (2) his work, all his life, has been graceful, even casual, not monumental. *Man* proved that Calder has all these years known the true extent of his own talent and pursued it carefully. In this one case the world's fair, instead of stimulating an artist to a new achievement, pushed him toward a vain and empty gesture.

Some of the buildings sited near *Man* were, seen purely as sculpture, far more effective; even the near bridge to the Ile Notre Dame had more aesthetic appeal. And this was true of Expo generally: the architects and engineers were better sculptors than the sculptors. Only in those few cases where sculptors worked closely with architects did they achieve anything remarkable: for instance in Irving Grossman's Press and Administration Building – the one Canadian building admired by nearly all the foreign architects – the use of sculptured walls by Ulysses Comtois, Ted Bieler and Armand Vaillancourt was superb. But at that building, near the edge of Expo, the good sculpture ended and the bad began. Right beside Grossman's building was a piece by Richard Turner, intended to symbolize electronic communications; it was a jumbled collection of images (an eye, some abstract wiring) that added up to the least impressive work of Turner's career. In this, Turner was not alone; many Canadian sculptors, having won considerable admiration for their work in the past, disappointed their admirers at Expo.

The fair commissioned some thirty-five pieces from Canadian sculptors, and of these no more than half a dozen – Robert Hedrick's, Robert Murray's, Michael Snow's were three – could be called distinguished. Gerald Gladstone, the most publicized and most praised of Canadian sculptors living in Canada, was represented at Expo by three major pieces, amounting to $200,000 in commissions: *Uki*, a fire-breathing monster at the Canadian pavilion; a large piece for the plaza sponsored by the engineers of Canada; and the largest single sculpture commissioned by Expo, a great artichoke-shaped piece at La Ronde. *Uki* was a great disappointment: a rusty, rather obvious collection of metal, it rose out of the water with great apparent difficulty and then did nothing much – even the children, who should have been its chief audience, weren't impressed. The engineers' sculpture was a kind of standard Gladstone, blown up to exposition size. The artichoke at La Ronde worked best, in a show-business sort of way, its combination of neon and concrete and water giving the area a sense of identity; but even here, it was less than Gladstone's admirers had expected.

The rest of the Canadian work suggested that Canadian sculptors, having earned their reputations mainly with art-gallery-sized pieces, weren't ready to adjust to monumental scale. On this level, like Alexander Calder, they grew pompous and empty. But perhaps there was a more serious reason than their lack of experience with monumental work. Perhaps Expo went shopping for the wrong kind of art at the wrong time. Expo looked for, and to some extent found, the kind of sculpture that involves humanistic shapes on the monumental scale. But by the middle 1960s sculpture was busy leaving humanism-with-monumentality behind. The kind of sculpture symbolized by Henry Moore (whose fine *Locking Piece* was well sited outside the British pavilion) was giving way, all around the world, to new concepts: various kinds of plastic sculpture, in which the spectator may become involved as a kind of participant; "environments," whole rooms designed to be walked through; minimal sculpture, in which ultra-simple and very solid-looking shapes replace the humanistic shapes of the Moore generation; and the kind of sculpture rep-

## A critic's collection of botched buildings

The author rated Man The Producer just a mass of rusty steel overpowering other buildings.

Air Canada's structure was meant to express flight, but the idea didn't get off the ground.

Inside, U.K.'s Pavilion was full of style; outside, "pretentious – a tent posing as a palace."

resented by the 1960s' British school, in which the object is reduced to thin abstract forms borrowed from industrial and construction techniques. None of this, or very little of it, was reflected at Expo, perhaps because so little of it has been either created or even shown in Canada.

Expo was in so many ways ahead of the times that it was never less than surprising to reflect that in this one area it was remarkably old-fashioned, tied to a set of artistic values that many good artists have abandoned as irrelevant.

Expo had some notable absentees, and these represented failures of a different kind. For some reason, Latin America was never sold on Expo – only Mexico, Cuba and Venezuela took part. A more important non-exhibitor was mainland China. As late as 1965 Pierre Dupuy said he hoped to bring in the Chinese; but he failed, and so one-third of the world's population was not represented at this "universal and international exhibition." The official excuse was that, since Canada doesn't officially recognize Peking, the Red Chinese couldn't be invited through normal diplomatic channels. This seemed odd to anyone who had noticed that a lack of diplomatic channels had not prevented Canada from selling the Chinese a few hundred million dollars' worth of wheat.

Expo never quite managed to sell itself to the Canadian business community. The telephone companies and the chemical companies participated handsomely, but the department stores, the soap manufacturers, the soft-drink companies and the food industry for the most part stayed out; and the car manufacturers, whose American parent companies contributed magnificently to the New York World's Fair in 1964-65, satisfied themselves with the contribution of a permanent outdoor stadium.

In at least one respect the content of Expo, outside of its own theme pavilions, was a disappointment. Expo was not, of course, an ordinary world's fair (perhaps there is no such thing), but it resembled other fairs rather more closely than its original planners hoped it would. The theme-setting conference of intellectuals at Montebello, Quebec, in 1963, recommended:

"The entire development of the Exhibition on the site shall reflect the primacy given to human values and aspirations in the theme 'Terre des Hommes'. It must not be presented as a 'Terre des nations' or a 'Terre des machines'."

But in the end, of course, the machinery often overshadowed the human beings, and the nations once more acted like nations – their pavilions were competitive, and no one tried to deny it. In this sense, Expo was a "Terre des nations." The original vision was thus lost or obscured. But perhaps that idea – international man as a display object taking precedence over the nation-state – was ahead of its time. Perhaps in the seventh decade of the 20th century the idea of nationalism was still an essential part of the idea of a world's fair.

# Sculpture to live with

Whether in park or pavilion, all Expo's sculpture was for people to experience, not just gaze upon, and much of it – like Peter Sager's splinter-free creation of wood at La Ronde Children's World – came alive when it was in use.

## Art to taunt, tempt, puzzle and haunt

Everyone got personally involved. Among the fifty sculptures in Ile Ste. Hélène rose garden, a man stoops to ask his own private question of a statue.

[*Above*] This girl seems almost envious of the "Palace Ladies Playing Polo": a pottery tableau from China's T'ang Dynasty (7th-8th century) displayed in the fine arts exhibition.

Art was to hold and handle: Germaine Richier's massive figure stoically supports a weary visitor as he checks the name plaque.

The earthy Auguste Rodin would have been amused by this girl's instinctive reaction to his figure displayed in the French Pavilion.

"La Pisana," by Italy's Arturo Martini: the sleeping girl captivated young and old.

## The work of art as a footbath

[*Left*] Gerald Gladstone's fountain at La Ronde – it was fondly called "the Artichoke" – was the work of art with which people became most involved. Officially entitled "Optical Orbital No. 2," it was a convenient place to bathe aching feet.

[*Below*] Michael Snow's "Walking Women" also had an extra asset: the reflective planes showed women if their hems were straight.

Russia-born Naum Gabo
sent the six-foot "Large Head."

Classic and contemporary,
Expo's sculpture spanned
4,000 years. Greece
showed figures
from her Golden Age.

Henry Moore's "Reclining
Figure With Pedestal"
reclined in the rose garden.

The message of Marino Marini's *Il Grido* – "The Scream" – seems to escape this child. She screamed all right – for mother.

[*Overleaf*] Alexander Calder's
67-foot "Man" appears as a
mind-bending nightmare
form, arising from the
beginnings of the world.

**His-and-her sculptures from France**

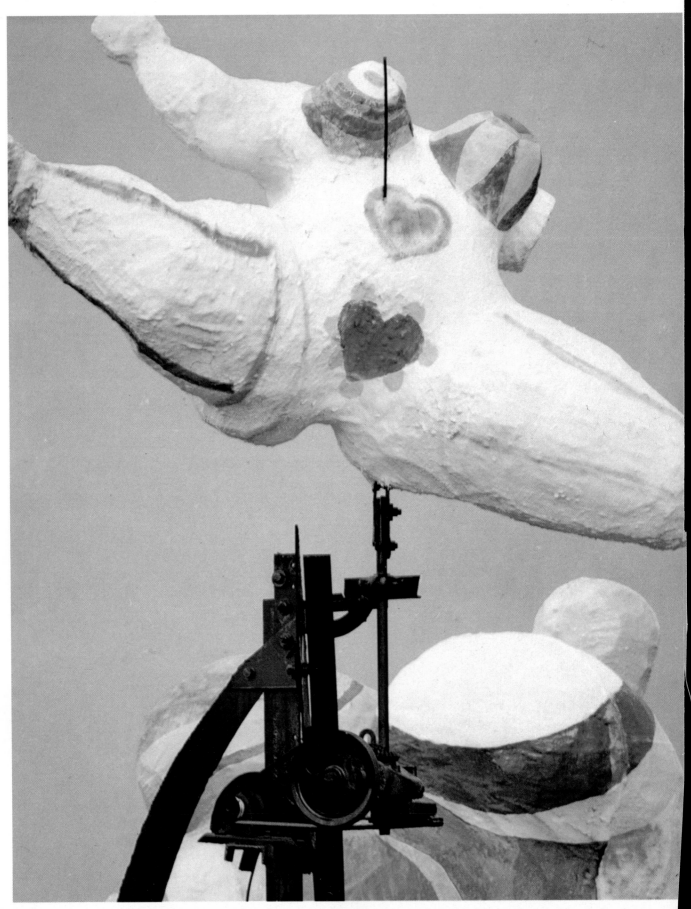

Mlle. Niki Sant Phalle's papier-mâché figures were impaled atop "art machines" by M. Jean Tinguely. Displayed on the roof
the French Pavilion, the figures symbolized passive female; the motor-driven clanking machines represented the active ma

# Epilogue  *A summer spent in the future*

For Canada and the world, Expo was a revelation. Everyone who came to see it, and millions more who only read about it, were brought into contact with new facts, new shapes, new ideas. Expo wasn't *quite* the most popular fair ever (Paris in 1900 had 50,860,801 visitors to Expo's 50,306,648), but it was probably the most widely discussed. The mass media, developed now as never before, carried its message around the world, and a German or a Californian or a Mexican who never went to Montreal could still learn a great deal about it.

There will never be a way to gauge accurately Expo's effect on the Canadian people. Certainly it brought them a new pride, but did it alter seriously their politics? Did Expo, which presented the Quebec people at their best, force English-speaking Canadians from other provinces to appreciate, finally, the vitality of the new French Canada? (For surely much of Expo's success was due to the great wave of energy released by Quebec's renewed sense of itself.) Did Expo, for that matter, cause French Canadians to recognize their connection with the rest of Canada, and perhaps even rejoice in it? We can hope so, of course, but we can never be sure.

We can understand, however – because the evidence grows steadily around us – the surge of confidence Expo produced in the hearts of Canadian artists. These people – film makers, designers, architects, whatever – complained for decades that their country never gave them a chance, never wanted to see what they could do. At Expo, they had their chance, they grasped it, and they impressed us profoundly. Good films, for instance, came from Czechoslovakia, the United States, and Britain, but none was better than the best of the Canadian films. That changed us.

But for Canadians and everyone else, this, finally, was the subject of Expo: Man, in his mind and imagination, has moved beyond scarcity. Man now has the knowledge to make a world of material comfort for every human creature on earth. We, the collective creators of our own world, can now feed everyone, can now house everyone, can now build modern cities of great beauty and high efficiency, can now distribute art and information to everyone. Science and technology have made all these things possible; but they remain, for now, only possibilities. Between the idea and the reality there still stands an army of problems – dead orthodoxies of nationalism and bureaucracy, of stunted imaginations and timid minds. Expo's function was to indicate the material and spiritual resources of the world of men, make them coherent, and show how we can use them if we have the courage to do so.

Expo 67 was the greatest birthday party in history, but for those willing to learn it was also an education. For one beautiful and unforgettable summer, Expo took us into the future that can be ours.

# Men who made the fair

Commissioner-General Pierre Dupuy

Deputy Commissioner Robert Shaw

Mayor of Montreal Jean Drapeau

Installations director
Colonel Edward Churchill

Operations director
Philippe de Gaspé Beaubien

The text for this book was set in
12 pt Times Roman by Mono Lino Limited
and the captions in 9 pt Helvetica
by Lino Composing Limited. The book was
printed in Canada by Rolph Clark
Stone Limited and binding
was done by T. H. Best Limited.

The texts for the picture stories in
this book were written by Alan Edmonds